WHY I STAND WITH ISRAEL

SEVEN REASONS TO SUPPORT
THE JEWISH STATE

McKade Marshall

This book is dedicated to the 6 million Jews who were systematically murdered by Nazis during the Holocaust between 1941 and 1945. The way we honor their lives is by never allowing such a genocide to ever take place again. We are now their voice. We must take action.

"McKade's unwavering, resolute passion for Israel and the Jewish people continues to both inform and inspire. Mozel Tov!"

ANDREW SUMMEY
Former Director of CUFI Students on Campus, Current Marketing Director of Zion Oil & Gas

"McKade has a love for God's people, and Israel is the first fruit of God's people! Read this book and learn about God's love for Israel! "

CLINT AND CHRISTI CHAPMAN
Pastors of Maranatha Fellowship (Albany, Texas)

Copyright © 2021 by McKade Marshall

All rights reserved. In accordance with the U.S. Copyright Act of 1976, the scanning, uploading, and electronic sharing of any part of this book without permission of the publisher is unlawful piracy and theft of the author's intellectual property. If you would like to use material from the book (other than for review purposes), prior written permission must be obtained by contacting the publisher. Thank you for your support of the author's rights.

Scripture quotations marked (ESV) are from the The Holy Bible, English Standard Version® (ESV®), copyright © 2001 by Crossway, a publishing ministry of Good News Publishers. Used by permission. All rights reserved.

Scripture quotations marked (NASB95) are taken from the New American Standard Bible®, Copyright © 1960, 1962, 1963, 1968, 1971, 1972, 1973, 1975, 1977, 1995 by The Lockman Foundation. Used by permission. (www.Lockman.org)

Scripture quotations marked (NCV) are taken from the New Century Version. Copyright © 2005 by Thomas Nelson, Inc. Used by permission. All rights reserved.

Scripture quotations marked (NIV) are taken from the Holy Bible, New International Version®, NIV®. Copyright © 1973, 1978, 1984, 2011 by Biblica, Inc.™ Used by permission of Zondervan. All rights reserved worldwide. www.zondervan.com The "NIV" and "New International Version" are trademarks registered in the United States Patent and Trademark Office by Biblica, Inc.™

Scripture quotations marked (NKJV) are taken from the New King James Version®. Copyright © 1982 by Thomas Nelson, Inc. Used by permission. All rights reserved.

Scripture quotations marked (NLT) are taken from the Holy Bible, New Living Translation, Copyright © 1996, 2004, 2007, 2013 by Tyndale House Foundation. Used by permission of Tyndale House Publishers, Inc., Carol Stream, Illinois 60188. All rights reserved.

MLM Publishing
PO Box 533
Malibu, CA 90265

www.mckademarshall.com

Printed in the United States of America

ISBN: 978-0-578-99027-9

Library of Congress Control Number: 2021947731

WHY I STAND WITH ISRAEL

Table of Contents

Introduction

Reason 1: God Tells Us To 13

Reason 2: Romans Eleven 43

Reason 3: Because Seeing is Believing 73

Reason 4: Israel is the Apple of God's Eye 103

Reason 5: Inwardly You are Jewish 133

Reason 6: Our True Allies in the Middle East 163

Reason 7: A Resilient People 193

Conclusion

Take Action

Introduction

I do not profess to be an expert on Jewish laws and customs or political affairs in the Middle East. I am sure there are others who have dedicated their lives to the study of the Middle East and modern conflict resolutions that could share with you a great deal more on the subject of Israel than I am going to share with you in this book. With that said, I do believe one of my greatest passions has always been supporting and defending the modern Jewish state of Israel. As a Christian, I find it almost impossible to not have a supernatural zeal for the well-being of the Holy Land - the land where Jesus Christ our Savior once walked, the land where many of the oracles of God were recorded and relayed from one generation to another, the land where God chose to make His name known.

Throughout history there has been a real hatred, an anti-Semitic spirit, against the Jewish people. It is most unfortunate. As believers, we know the devil hates anything that is from God. The Scriptures tell us concerning the devil in John 8:44 (ESV), "He was a murderer from the beginning, and does not stand in the truth, because there is no truth in him. When he lies, he speaks out of his own character, for he is a liar and the father of lies." The last thing the enemy wants is for God's people to thrive. He hates Israel, and he hates God's church establishment. Why? Because both Israel and the church of God are a testament to the truth. The Jewish people are the ones God chose to use to give the Law of Moses and later to birth the coming Messiah, Who is in the generational line of Judah. The church is the administration God has chosen to use to declare the gospel to the ends of the earth in these last days (see Acts 1:8).

I am really excited to share with you my fourth book Why I Stand With Israel: 7 Reasons to Support the Jewish State. For several years I have planned to write about why it is so important to stand with Israel. Having been raised in the church and taught the Scriptures virtually from the womb, I have always known there is something spiritually significant and profound about a tiny spot on the world map called "Israel". What is perhaps even more intriguing about this small country is it was established as the State of Israel on May 14, 1948. Given that the last Jewish state to exist was some 2,000 years ago, this is a remarkable recent event in history to witness and be a part of.

I believe what we are seeing today with the current affairs happening in and around the State of Israel is nothing less than prophecy from Scriptures actively in motion. God has told us through the prophet Isaiah that His Word will not return to Him empty (Isaiah 55:11). What God has spoken over Israel since the beginning of its creation thousands of years ago is still at work today. The prophet Isaiah declares in Isaiah 40:8 (NLT), "The grass withers and the flowers fade, but the word of our God stands forever," and Jesus tells us in Matthew 24:35, "Heaven and earth will pass away, but My words will never pass away."

What has been spoken and recorded in the Bible is engraved permanently in stone. God's Word lasts forever. We can believe and stand on His Word for all we are ever going to need in life. The same is eternally true regarding all things God has spoken concerning the nation of Israel. As I share with you why I support Israel, the root of my immovable stance is all based on what the Bible says. One might argue with me about my views on Israel. One might develop their own opinions towards what I think about this country, as it often comes up in hot political debates. However, for the believer, no one can refute what God has already said concerning Israel in His Word.

If Israel mattered to Jesus two millennia ago, then Israel should also matter to His church today. You are a member of Christ's body - a body that is established upon what happened on the cross of Calvary which is outside the gates of Jerusalem in the Jewish homeland. Jesus' blood is what unites Jews and Gentiles into one people (Ephesians 2:14). Seeing all people given the opportunity to step into Christ's kingdom was God's plan from the beginning. While it was the Jewish people who turned Jesus over to be crucified, it was Gentile soldiers who nailed Him to the cross. All the world is guilty of sin. We all need redemption. This redemption can only happen through an Israelite named Jesus.

I pray that as you read each reason to support the Jewish state of Israel your faith rises to take action. In my personal life, I have had the opportunity to travel and partner with different ministries and political organizations to help further the well-being of Israel and the Jewish people. I look forward to sharing some of these experiences and life-changing moments throughout the book. While we may not all have the once-in-a-lifetime opportunity to physically visit the land of Israel, we are all still spiritually connected to the homeland of our Lord and Savior Jesus Christ.

As you read each section I encourage you to begin making it a habit to pray for Israel. Israel is where God chose to place His name. The new covenant began in Israel, and the end of all earthly things will conclude in Israel. What happens in Israel dictates the direction of the world. Israel is the geographical centerpiece of the globe. The modern rebirth of Israel after World War II is a testament to God's mercy and redemptive grace. The physical wars we see surrounding this magnificent land today are merely a reflection of the war taking place in the spiritual realm. It is up to us, God's people, to pray Israel through these incredible spiritual battles.

Expect to be blessed in your personal life as you pray for and stand with God's chosen nation. The Lord is certainly not finished with the diaspora of Israel. He is now once again calling His people home. As we witness more and more Jewish families return to the Jewish state, I believe there is going to be an outpouring of the Holy Spirit across the earth, over both Jews and Gentiles alike, like we have never seen before, until all of God's people become one through Christ Jesus. Thus, the Scriptures will be fulfilled which say, "But you are a chosen race, a royal priesthood, a holy nation, a people for His own possession, that you may proclaim the excellencies of Him who called you out of darkness into His marvelous light." (1 Peter 2:9 ESV)

REASON ONE

God Tells Us To

As believers, we should live and make decisions based on what the Scriptures tell us. The Bible is our operating manual for life. The texts are recordings throughout history made by people moved by the Spirit of God. The Apostle Paul tells the church in 2 Timothy 3:15-17 (NLT), "You have been taught the holy Scriptures from childhood, and they have given you the wisdom to receive the salvation that comes by trusting in Christ Jesus. All Scripture is inspired by God and is useful to teach us what is true and to make us realize what is wrong in our lives. It corrects us when we are wrong and teaches us to do what is right. God uses it to prepare and equip His people to do every good work."

Everything we believe is subject to the Word of God. It is our go-to guide for all matters pertaining to godly living. How we feel today and the things we have experienced in the past all play a part in how we think, operate, and make decisions on a daily basis. However, no matter what is going on in our mind, will, and emotions, everything we process and believe is subject to what God says. Hebrews 4:12 (NASB95) says, "For the word of God is living and active and sharper than any two-edged sword, and piercing as far as the division of soul and spirit, of both joints and marrow, and able to judge the thoughts and intentions of the heart." The Holy Bible is God's gift to us. He has preserved His Word for thousands of years to ensure all people might come to know Him as their Creator and Savior.

Jesus Christ is the Word of God. Revelation 19:13 (NASB95) says, "His name is called The Word of God." When God speaks, there is a myriad of angels following that word to ensure His will is carried out (Psalm 103:20). Everything God says is intentional and eternal. He is not like people. If you have ever turned on the TV and watched a talk show, there is a lot of chatter. Careless words are thrown here and there. Opinions and viewpoints from "experts" abound on radio shows, podcasts, and streaming videos. With so many voices in the world today, it can be easy to think truth is more obscure than absolute.

However, truth is not an opinion. Truth is fact. Truth is the reality of how things really are. When it comes to spiritual matters, we do not get to pick and choose which parts of Scripture we want to listen to. The entire Bible, from Genesis to Revelation, is relevant to our walks with God. God is the Word so if we want to know Him we need to know His Word. If God's Word says to bless the nation of Israel, then we are to bless Israel. Whether we understand why we are to bless Israel or not is less important than actually doing it because God has said to. Our obedience to His Word is what causes us to have a deeper understanding as to why He has commanded us to do it in the first place.

Psalm 111:10 (NASB95) tells us, "The fear of the LORD is the beginning of wisdom; A good understanding have all those who do His commandments; His praise endures forever." There is a fountain of wisdom and understanding that is unlocked when we obey God's commandments. One of the first commands we are given in the Scriptures is to bless Israel. Genesis 12:3 (NASB95) says, "And I will bless those who bless you, And the one who curses you I will curse. And in you all the families of the earth will be blessed." If you desire to see more of God's goodness in your life and in the lives of your loved ones then it's time to start blessing Israel.

I have seen the supernatural blessings of God first hand from blessing Israel. A few years ago I felt led to invest financially into the wellbeing of Israel. That summer I had extra funds and was praying about what to do with them. When the opportunity came to invest, it's like the floodgates of heaven opened up in my finances. Business picked up. New doors of opportunity opened. Almost overnight I went to a whole new level in resources and provision after I invested in Israel. Today I am still walking in the blessings and opportunities that opened up that summer.

Investing in Israel was a step of faith. I did not know how God would bless me, but I knew He promised that He would. Over the course of the next several weeks I came across new opportunities to grow. Knowledge I didn't have before came across my path, which helped me make wiser decisions for the future. What happened? Was this all just a coincidence? I don't think it was. I believe one reason I saw such a level of increase is because I first sowed into and blessed the nation God chose to make His name great through. I used what little I had in my hand believing God could do more than I could ever do in my own strength.

The same can be true for you. When you honor God and you honor the land He has chosen to send His Son Jesus, the one true Messiah, through to bring salvation to the world, then get ready to experience God's goodness and favor in a whole new way. There is a God-ordained, commanded blessing on your life for sowing into the Holy Land. The Lord chose Israel and the Jewish people to relay the very oracles of God in Heaven for the entire world to hear about, read, and study throughout the ages (Romans 3:2). The church and Christian doctrine are founded upon events that primarily happened in and around the land of Israel.

The blessing on the land of Israel is irrevocable. The Lord promises over and over throughout the Scriptures to give the land we know as Israel to the direct descendants of Abraham, Isaac, and Jacob for all time. These descendants are the Jewish people. The Lord tells Jacob in a vision in Genesis 28:13-14 (NIV), "I am the LORD, the God of your father Abraham and the God of Isaac. I will give you and your descendants the land on which you are lying. Your descendants will be like the dust of the earth, and you will spread out to the west and to the east, to the north and to the south. All peoples on earth will be blessed through you and your offspring."

Without the Jewish people, the world would be lost and hopeless. As Jesus tells the Samaritan woman at the well, "You Samaritans know very little about the One you worship, while we Jews know all about Him, for salvation comes through the Jews." (John 4:22 NLT) The Apostle Paul reiterates this powerful truth when He addresses the early church saying in Ephesians 2:11-12 (NLT), "Don't forget that you Gentiles used to be outsiders. You were called 'uncircumcised heathens' by the Jews, who were proud of their circumcision, even though it affected only their bodies and not their hearts. In those days you were living apart from Christ. You were excluded from citizenship among the people of Israel, and you did not know the covenant promises God had made to them. You lived in this world without God and without hope." In other words, before Jesus was born much of the world was far away from God. Most of the Gentile nations served and worshipped pagan gods.

The good news is God has brought all people groups and all nations close to Him through Jesus Christ. The Lord has not just disclosed Himself to the Israelites only but to all nations. We are living in a time of prophetic fulfillment. We have the opportunity to walk in and experience the living Word of God when we accept the free gift of Christ's salvation. The prophet Joel declares in Joel 2:27-29 (ESV), "You shall know that I am in the midst of Israel, and that I am the LORD your God and there is none else. And My people shall never again be put to shame. And it shall come to pass afterward, that I will pour out My Spirit on all flesh; your sons and your daughters shall prophesy, your old men shall dream dreams, and your young men shall see visions. Even on the male and female servants in those days I will pour out My Spirit." (See also Acts 2:14-18)

Through Jesus and the promised Holy Spirit that has come down out of Heaven Jews and Gentiles have now been merged together as one under the banner of Christ's love. The Apostle Paul explains in Ephesians 2:14-15 (NLT) saying, "For Christ Himself has brought peace to us. He united Jews and Gentiles into one people when, in His own body on the cross, He broke down the wall of hostility that separated us. He did this by ending the system of Law with its commandments and regulations. He made peace between Jews and Gentiles by creating in Himself one new people from the two groups." We are living an era of divine restoration. Not only is the Lord drawing both Jews and Gentiles close, but He is also restoring the nation of Israel back to its place of leadership in the current world order.

The Lord has shown me through the Scriptures and by what I am seeing happening in the Middle East today that He is coming back soon. One night while I was listening to worship music and resting on my bed I began to have a vision from the Lord. In this vision I saw Jesus floating over the Holy Land. I remember the rolling hills and fertile plains of Israel from when I had visited during my college days and recognized the geography I was seeing. In the vision I started to see seven stars come out of the heavens, and they began swirling all over and around the nation of Israel. Jesus was in the midst of them and was causing the stars to follow one another until they took their place in the sky.

At first I did not understand the vision. For the next few nights I continued to see the same vision before I fell asleep. The seven stars continued to swirl over Israel in the darkness of the night every time. It was a very peaceful and comforting vision before bedtime. Then one day it occurred to me the meaning of the vision God kept showing me. The number seven represents completion in the Bible. The stars represent God restoring the nation of Israel to completion during these last days before the great tribulation and then the 1,000-year reign of Christ. The stars also represent the seven churches mentioned in chapters 2 and 3 in the book of Revelation. Looking back now I also realize the seven stars over Israel represent the seven reasons I support the Jewish state of Israel today. Hence, a "7-7-7" revelation if you will!

While I believe the church today will be raptured from the earth before the Great Tribulation of 7 years begins (an in-depth study of the book of Daniel, the gospels, and Revelation are what have led me to this strong belief), I also believe the 1,000-year reign of Christ over the entire world will be from the literal land of Israel today (before the new heaven and the new earth replace the earth we now see). This all seems mind-boggling and far out, but if we can look at modern day Israel and see Jesus literally coming back one day to sit on His rightful throne where Jerusalem is now, it will only strengthen our faith in supporting Israel when she is under fire by so many around her!

The Apostle John tells us in Revelation 20:4 (ESV), "I saw the souls of those who had been beheaded for the testimony of Jesus and for the word of God, and those who had not worshiped the beast or its image and had not received its mark on their foreheads or their hands. They came to life and reigned with Christ for a thousand years." The Apostle John goes on to say in Revelation 20:5-6 (ESV), "The rest of the dead did not come to life until the thousand years were ended. This is the first resurrection. Blessed and holy is the one who shares in the first resurrection! Over such the second death has no power, but they will be priests of God and of Christ, and they will reign with him for a thousand years."

I believe it is important to realize the magnitude of what is happening today in Israel. It all leads to the final chapters of the time period we are in. God has commanded us to bless this chosen nation. Some may argue that the Old Testament law no longer applies under the new covenant, and therefore God's blessing on literal Israel today is obsolete (see Hebrews 8:13). However, when people who argue the broken old covenant is no longer valid (which the prophet Jeremiah said would be superseded by a new and better covenant in Jeremiah 31:31-35 through Christ) they are forgetting God made His promise to Abraham before the Mosaic law was ever enacted. The promise God made to Abraham and his bloodline concerning the land of Israel is forever. It did not go away when Christ came to enact the new covenant based on better promises (see Hebrews 8:6).

One of the leading passages of Scripture that reveal just how close we are to Christ's Second Coming is in Luke 21:24 (NASB95), when Jesus tells His disciples, "And the Jewish people will fall by the edge of the sword, and will be led captive into all the nations; and Jerusalem will be trampled under foot by the Gentiles until the times of the Gentiles are fulfilled." Folks, Jerusalem is no longer being trampled over by the Gentiles. Israel once again belongs to the Jewish people. Praise the Lord! When Jesus made this prophetic statement, He was prophesying about both the coming destruction of Jerusalem in 70 AD by the Roman military and then the restoration of the Jewish state of Israel on May 14, 1948.

Nobody knows the exact day or hour Jesus is returning (Matthew 24:36). However, like Noah the ark builder, the people of God should be busy building God's kingdom when He finally does return. As the church, we have the opportunity to bless the nation of Israel. Now more than ever the church should support Israel, as she is under fire in all directions. The reason Israel is under so much attack is because in the unseen spiritual realm, Satan and his entire demonic army are trying to destroy her. The Apostle John explains in Revelation 12:13 (NKJV), "Now when the dragon saw that he had been cast to the earth, he persecuted the woman who gave birth to the male Child." The verses before and after make it obvious who these different character references are. The dragon represents Satan, the woman represents Israel, or the Jewish people, and the male Child is Jesus who was born as a descendant of Israel.

Revelation 12:13 tells us the devil persecutes Israel to this day, as Israel is where salvation to the world has come. Israel is where Satan and his rebellious dominion have been overcome through Jesus Christ our Lord! If you ever wonder why so many people hate Israel and the Jewish people seemingly without a cause, which is called anti-Semitism, you no longer need to. Revelation 12:13 tells us why. The devil hates Israel; therefore, he will do everything in his power to convince anyone who is not following God to hate Israel too. I have been caught off guard so many times when I hear "Christians" speak with malice towards Israel and the Jewish people. Not to be too blunt, but this kind of thinking is satanic by nature.

Even the Apostle Paul, who was continually beaten and pursued by unbelieving Jewish religious leaders, refused to give up on his own countrymen. Paul says in Romans 9:1-5 (NLT), "With Christ as my witness, I speak with utter truthfulness. My conscience and the Holy Spirit confirm it. My heart is filled with bitter sorrow and unending grief for my people, my Jewish brothers and sisters. I would be willing to be forever cursed—cut off from Christ!—if that would save them. They are the people of Israel, chosen to be God's adopted children. God revealed His glory to them. He made covenants with them and gave them His law. He gave them the privilege of worshiping Him and receiving His wonderful promises. Abraham, Isaac, and Jacob are their ancestors, and Christ Himself was an Israelite as far as His human nature is concerned. And He is God, the One who rules over everything and is worthy of eternal praise! Amen."

Then again, Jesus Himself grieved over the Jewish people rejecting Him as God's promised Messiah and Savior of the world as well. He says in Luke 13:34 (ESV), "O Jerusalem, Jerusalem, the city that kills the prophets and stones those who are sent to it! How often would I have gathered your children together as a hen gathers her brood under her wings, and you were not willing!" It is clear from the Scriptures the magnitude of importance and even prominence Israel holds in the eyes of God. However, knowing how much God values Israel should not cause us to automatically undervalue any other nation or people group. God is not willing that any should perish! (2 Peter 3:9) God's will is not just that Israel would be saved, but that all people would come to know Him. King David declares in Psalm 86:9 (NASB95), "All nations whom You have made shall come and worship before You, O Lord, and they shall glorify Your name."

Today people from nations all around the world gather every week at church to celebrate what Christ has done on the Cross. We have been given freedom from the shackles of sin and death through His blood (Romans 7:24-25). If we could begin to grasp just how much God loves us, if that were even possible, then we might understand how much God loves Israel also in the present day. Deuteronomy 7:6-7 (ESV) says, "For you are a people holy to the LORD your God. The LORD your God has chosen you to be a people for His treasured possession, out of all the peoples who are on the face of the earth. It was not because you were more in number than any other people that the LORD set His love on you and chose you, for you were the fewest of all peoples." God chose Israel not because of its strength or size, but because of His covenant with Abraham, Isaac, and Jacob. He chose Israel by His own divine choice.

We are living in a time when the Jewish people are re-entering the Promised Land God promised to them several millennia ago. If we want to experience more of God's goodness and blessings in our own lives, one way we can expand the scope of our faith in serving the Lord is by praying for and even participating with organizations that support Israel. There is a supernatural commanded blessing on the lives of you and your family when you step out in faith and back Israel. In the Scriptures, God caused the surrounding nations to tremble before Israel as He led them into the land of Canaan (also called "Palestine"). The Lord went with His people in order to drive out the inhabitants in the land who were not living right.

This same principle is still true today. If you observe the Middle East, there are some very serious issues. Terror groups and false religions (like the different sects of Islam) dominate the regions. While we should pray for the salvation of people living in the Middle East (and I certainly do!), we also need to be aware that in the unseen realm God has a way of bringing justice to those who refuse to honor the One True God. One reason Islam dominates this area is because of Ishmael and his descendants. Ishmael was the first child of Abraham who was born to his mistress Hagar. However, Ishmael was not the promised child. The Lord told Abraham it would be through his wife Sarah that the promised child would come.

When Sarah finally had Isaac in her old age, she had had enough of Hagar and her son Ishmael. Genesis 21:9-10 (NLT) tells us, "But Sarah saw Ishmael—the son of Abraham and her Egyptian servant Hagar—making fun of her son, Isaac. So she turned to Abraham and demanded, 'Get rid of that slave woman and her son. He is not going to share the inheritance with my son, Isaac. I won't have it!'" Seeing as to how Ishmael was both 14 years older than Isaac and not the promised child God had given to Abraham from her, Sarah had no tolerance for Ishmael picking on Isaac. Deeply distressed, Abraham reluctantly sends Hagar and Ishmael away after the Lord tells him He would make Ishmael's descendants a great nation too.

It is through the descendants of Ishmael that Muhammad, the prophet of Islam, traces his lineage. While this is not directly stated in the Bible, Muhammad traces his lineage all the way back to Nebaioth, who is the firstborn son of Ishmael (see Genesis 25:12-18). Today we see a spiritual truth at work that started all the way back with the sons of Hagar and Sarah. The Apostle Paul tells the church in Galatians 4:28-31 (NIV), "Now you, brothers and sisters, like Isaac, are children of promise. At that time the son born according to the flesh persecuted the son born by the power of the Spirit. It is the same now. But what does Scripture say? 'Get rid of the slave woman [Hagar] and her son [Ishmael], for the slave woman's son will never share in the inheritance with the free woman's son [Isaac].' Therefore, brothers and sisters, we are not children of the slave woman, but of the free woman [Sarah]."

Just as Ishmael persecuted Isaac because he was the one chosen by God, so those who practice Islamic terrorism persecute Jews and Christians today also. The good news is anyone can be a child of the free woman (allegorically speaking) through Jesus Christ our Lord! Jesus came to redeem Jews, Muslims, Christians, non-Christians, Buddhists, Hindus, atheists, and anyone who will receive Him. The gospel means good news for anyone who believes in Jesus' name. Jesus is the only way to eternal salvation. The Lord tells His disciples in Matthew 7:13-15 (NIV), "Enter through the narrow gate. For wide is the gate and broad is the road that leads to destruction, and many enter through it. But small is the gate and narrow the road that leads to life, and only a few find it. Watch out for false prophets. They come to you in sheep's clothing, but inwardly they are ferocious wolves."

Right now I challenge you to stop for a second and think about how many different religions and ideologies there are in this world. It is estimated there are around 4,200 different religions in existence today. While Christianity dominates as the largest religion on the planet (followed by Islam), there are still many different paths a person can choose to follow in this life. Jesus tells us there is only a small gate, a narrow path, that a person can take in order to have eternal life. This narrow path is narrow because there is only one gate. Jesus Christ is the gate. Apart from Christ, all other roads lead to destruction. As time goes on, more and more people will reject this Biblical truth. The idea that there is only one way to heaven will be rejected by the majority (if it is not already).

The same is true with the nation of Israel. The day is coming when all nations will turn against Israel. All peoples who come against Jerusalem will bring infliction only upon themselves. The prophet Zechariah declares in Zechariah 12:3 (NLT), "On that day I will make Jerusalem an immovable rock. All the nations will gather against it to try to move it, but they will only hurt themselves." How many countries already are trying to usurp Israel's right to claim Jerusalem as its capital? As time progresses, the attacks on Israel will only increase. Why? Because in these last days people's hearts will grow cold towards God (see Matthew 24:12). 2 Chronicles 6:5-6 (NIV) says, "Since the day I brought My people out of Egypt, I have not chosen a city in any tribe of Israel to have a temple built so that My Name might be there, nor have I chosen anyone to be ruler over My people Israel. But now I have chosen Jerusalem for My Name to be there, and I have chosen David to rule My people Israel."

God has placed His name on the land of Israel. One of the interpretations of the name Israel is "Prince with God". After Jacob wrestled with an angel all night and prevailed, God renamed Jacob "Israel" (Genesis 32:28). Through Jacob, or Israel, the Prince of Peace came to the earth. The Prince of Peace, that is Jesus, established peace between God and man (Romans 5:1). It should come as no surprise that peace with God for the entire world was established in the city of Jerusalem when Jesus gave up His life on the cross as the Lamb of God. Jerusalem is the eternal capital of Israel and the city of David. It is the city of God. It only makes sense that the Son of God would come to redeem all people from sin in the very city God's temple was built.

What happens now in Jerusalem is just as important today as it was 2,000 years ago. This is why we should always be praying for the peace of Jerusalem. What happens in Jerusalem impacts the entire world. One day the enemy of God, that is the anti-Christ, will seat himself on the throne of God and declare himself to be God. The Apostle Paul explains in 2 Thessalonians 2:3-4 (NASB95) saying, "Let no one in any way deceive you, for it [the day Jesus returns to earth a second time] will not come unless the apostasy [many walking away from the faith] comes first, and the man of lawlessness is revealed, the son of destruction, who opposes and exalts himself above all that is called God or that is worshiped, so that he sits as God in the temple of God, showing himself that he is God." Brothers and sisters, the day for the enemy to seat himself in Jerusalem and declare himself to be God is drawing very close.

The only reason the devil has not come in human form and declared himself to be God is because God's power is restraining him. It is the Holy Spirit and Christ's church that is holding the devil back from deceiving the whole world. If this does not alarm the church it should! 2 Thessalonians 2:6-7 (NLT) says, "And you know what is holding him [the anti-Christ] back, for he can be revealed only when his time comes. For this lawlessness is already at work secretly, and it will remain secret until the one who is holding it back steps out of the way." When the Lord takes back his restraining hand, the devil will temporarily get what he has always wanted (or so he thinks), which is to be worshipped as God (Isaiah 14:13-14). The Bible tells us that God will even allow this lawless man to display false signs and wonders to deceive the whole world.

The Apostle Paul goes on to tell the church in 2 Thessalonians 2:9-12 (ESV), "The coming of the lawless one is by the activity of Satan with all power and false signs and wonders, and with all wicked deception for those who are perishing, because they refused to love the truth and so be saved. Therefore God sends them a strong delusion, so that they may believe what is false, in order that all may be condemned who did not believe the truth but had pleasure in unrighteousness." The belief that the man of lawlessness is God come in the flesh is the strong delusion the Lord is going to allow the world to be under, because it refused to accept the truth and love of God. The man of lawlessness to be revealed is the exact opposite of Jesus, the Son of God, come in the flesh.

The good news is when these two opposing men, one born of God and one born of the devil, meet face to face, there is no contest. 2 Thessalonians 2:8 (ESV) tells us, "And then the lawless one will be revealed, whom the Lord Jesus will kill with the breath of His mouth and bring to nothing by the appearance of His coming." One breath and the anti-Christ is toast in the presence of the King of all kings! Jesus is all-powerful; He carries the keys of death and hell. The devil has no room to exist in the presence of our Savior. The same is true in your own life. When you declare the name of Jesus, the devil must flee. Darkness and light cannot co-exist. When you turn the light on, darkness is immediately dispelled.

No matter how many counterfeit tricks the devil tries to play on you, God's Word stops them all. God says that no weapon formed against you is going to prosper. We have this promise because it is a promise that was originally made to the nation of Israel many years ago. In Isaiah 54:17 (NASB95), the prophet Isaiah declares, "'No weapon that is formed against you will prosper; and every tongue that accuses you in judgment you will condemn. This is the heritage of the servants of the LORD, and their vindication is from Me,' declares the LORD." When Isaiah made this promise from the Lord, he was addressing a Jewish audience. However, it was also prophetic for all the Gentiles who were to be grafted into the promises of God also through the Messiah. The reason I bring this up is because as believers we need to realize the foundations of our faith are deeply rooted in our Jewish ancestors of the faith.

God chose the Jewish people to display His glory to the world. He did not ask us if we thought this was fair. He did not ask us if we thought He should choose Israel, a country the size of New Jersey, to bring forth salvation to the world. If God commands His church to bless Israel, and He certainly does, then we are to bless it. For those who might disagree, I believe the Lord has made His case through His Word. It is foolish to try to tell God how we think things ought to be, that somehow we know more than He does. The Lord rhetorically asks Job, in Job 38:4-7 (NCV), saying, "Where were you when I made the earth's foundation? Tell me, if you understand. Who marked off how big it should be? Surely you know! Who stretched a ruler across it? What were the earth's foundations set on, or who put its cornerstone in place while the morning stars sang together and all the angels shouted with joy?"

Israel is a nation built several millennia ago. What's even more profound is Israel came into existence because of angels, under the command of God in Heaven, who visited the forefathers of our faith. Anyone who comes against the people of Israel, beware. You are warring against God's holy angels. The Scriptures say God's Law and commands have been ordained through His angels (Acts 7:53). These angels steward the Word of God at all times to ensure everything God has spoken from His throne comes to pass (Psalm 103:20). When you pray for Israel, these angels are listening to what you have to say. They are ministering spirits from Heaven sent to watch over God's people (Hebrews 1:14).

We are living in a time period very similar to the time when Israel was entering the Promised Land, being led by Joshua, in the Old Testament. The Lord has gathered Jewish men and women from all over the world and has brought them home. We are witnessing a modern-day miracle!

I believe a great revival, a global scale spiritual harvest, is coming as we begin to see Israel be restored in a way like never seen before in history. As the Hebrew people take back all the land that rightfully belongs to them, all the nations of the earth are going to be blessed. Those who stand in the way are going to be struck with a holy terror from the Lord. This is exactly what happened in the Old Testament when God tells Moses that He is going to drive out the inhabitants of the land because they were evil. The Lord tells Moses in Exodus 23:27-30 (NLT), "I will send My terror ahead of you and create panic among all the people whose lands you invade. I will make all your enemies turn and run. I will send terror ahead of you to drive out the Hivites, Canaanites, and Hittites. But I will not drive them out in a single year, because the land would become desolate and the wild animals would multiply and threaten you. I will drive them out a little at a time until your population has increased enough to take possession of the land."

What's so profound about this passage of Scripture is that this is what is happening today in Israel. Since the horrific Holocaust, little by little Israel has regained control of its land over the ensuing decades. The Israel Defense Force (IDF) is now stronger than ever and is a militant power to be reckoned with. The Bible ensures us that God is just as much with the Israeli army today is He was over 3,000 years ago when He went before Joshua driving out the inhabitants of the land. It is important that as Christians we understand why God drove out the people who lived in Canaan in the Old Testament in the first place and also why He is likely doing the same thing today. The Bible says in Deuteronomy 9:4 (NIV), "It is on account of the wickedness of these nations that the LORD is going to drive them out before you."

The biggest opponent of Israel and the Jewish people possessing the land of Israel today is the Muslims. The largest false religion in existence today (Islam) is being used by Satan to try and keep the Jewish people from inhabiting the land that has belong to them since God made His covenant with Abraham in Genesis. Muslim (Arab) nations believe the land is Muslim lands. However, we as the church should know better. The land has been deeded by Almighty God to the children of Abraham, Isaac, and Jacob as an everlasting covenant. Genesis 17:8 (NIV) tells us, "The whole land of Canaan, where you now reside as a foreigner, I will give as an everlasting possession to you and your descendants after you; and I will be their God." Another translation says the land would be given as an "eternal" possession to the Jewish people.

While God has allowed the Jewish people to be scattered around the world, He still has not forsaken His covenant with Abraham. Since God's promise to Abraham, the land has always belonged to the Hebrew people. Throughout the Babylonian exile, throughout the diaspora after Jerusalem's destruction in 70 AD, and throughout any other time period following God's promise to Abraham, the land has always belonged to the Jewish people. Now the Hebrew people actually possessing the land is another story. God has allowed the Hebrews to temporarily be removed from their homeland because of their turning away from Him. However, the land still belongs to them. It is a promise from God that cannot be revoked! (Romans 11:29)

As we are living in a time when Jews have and are still re-entering the Promised Land, we have the opportunity to be a blessing to Israel. We have the opportunity to receive a blessing for being a blessing. We have the privilege as children of God to begin to partner with and co-labor with the Lord in what He is doing in the Middle East. However, I have noticed there are some people, even people who attend church each week, who carry a strong bias against Israel and the Jewish people. Instead of defending the Israelis who are on guard against their enemies 24/7 on every side, they are defending the ones who are trying to take Israel off the map.

I do not understand their bias against Israel except that they have been misled about the truth. In the book of Numbers, a prophet by the name of Balaam was paid to curse Israel by the king of Moab. Balak, the Moabite king, saw what the Spirit-led, Israelite army had done to the Amorites and knew this God-favored army was headed straight for him. Instead of repenting or trying to seek the one true God of Israel, Balak goes to the elders, and they gather money to seek a diviner who would curse the Jews for them. Balak sends messengers to Balaam, and says in Numbers 22:6 (NLT), "Please come and curse these people for me because they are too powerful for me. Then perhaps I will be able to conquer them and drive them from the land. I know that blessings fall on any people you bless, and curses fall on people you curse."

The hostility towards Israel today is just as great as it was all the way back in the book of Numbers. If we are not careful, we can begin to only look at things from the outside in - that is, to only consider what the physical eye can see with no consideration for what is happening in the spiritual realm. As Christians, we need to realize that the hand of God is what led Israel into the land of Canaan thousands of years ago. Today it is still the same hand of God that has led the Jewish people back to their homeland and created the Jewish state of Israel. When Balaam goes to prophesy over

Israel, he warns Balak that he would only speak what God tells him to speak. He tells Balaam in Numbers 22:18 (NASB95), "Though Balak were to give me his house full of silver and gold, I could not do anything, either small or great, contrary to the command of the LORD my God."

Balak continues to persist that Balaam come to him and curse Israel. After the prophet Balaam is rebuked by a talking donkey, which God caused to speak (read Numbers 22:22-35), the Moabite king takes Balaam to a high place of Baal (who is their false god) where some of the Israelites could be seen nearby; Balak prepares a sacrifice at the prophet's instruction. When the prophet Balaam returns after communing with God about what to say, he begins to prophesy over Israel. He declares in Numbers 23:7-9 (NIV), "Balak brought me from Aram, the king of Moab from the eastern mountains. 'Come,' he said, 'curse Jacob for me; come, denounce Israel.' How can I curse those whom God has not cursed? How can I denounce those whom the Lord has not denounced? From the rocky peaks I see them, from the heights I view them. I see a people who live apart and do not consider themselves one of the nations."

What's interesting about this prophesy Balaam makes is he says Israel is not like the surrounding nations. The same is still true today. In the Middle East Israel is surrounded by 22 Arab nations. These Arab nations possess around 650 times more territory than Israel and are cumulatively about 50 times greater than Israel in population. When God chose Israel to be blessed, even the highly reputable prophet Balaam could not put a curse on them. The same is true now. Even if the church were to turn its back on Israel (God forbid!), Almighty God would still thwart all their enemies. The only time God has allowed Israel to suffer serious harm is when they have forsaken Him. Even then, God has still kept His promise made to Abraham that the land would always belong to Israel. When Jesus came to usher in a new covenant of grace, He did not cancel this promised deed to Abraham and his literal Jewish descendants. Jesus prophesied the Jews would be scattered for a period of time, but then they would be drawn back to their homeland (Luke 21:24).

When Balaam blessed Israel the first time, King Balak was dismayed. The king had another idea since Balaam already blessed a portion of the Jews down below. He tells the prophet in Numbers 23:13 (NIV), "Come with me to another place where you can see them; you will not see them all but only the outskirts of their camp. And from there, curse them for me." They build another altar and Balaam seeks the Lord again to deliver the next prophetic word. The prophet then declares to Balak in Numbers 23:18-20 (NLT), "Rise up, Balak, and listen! Hear me, son of Zippor. God is not a man, so He does not lie. He is not human, so He does not change His mind. Has He ever spoken and failed to act? Has He ever promised and not carried it through? Listen, I received a command to bless; God has blessed, and I cannot reverse it!"

Friends, it is impossible to reverse the blessing on the Jewish state of Israel. The Lord has not changed His mind. Unfortunately, we have some modern-day Moabites who do not realize they are cursing what God has already blessed. Like with Balaam and the talking donkey, God may need to send an angel to correct the church! There is no place for anti-Semitism among God's people. The anti-Semitic spirit we now see in the world is clearly a demonic spirit. When Hitler rounded up the Jewish people, devising Holocaust trains to transport them to concentration camps, he was clearly under a very demonic, anti-Semitic spirit from hell. There are still millions of people in the world today (if not billions) who hate the Jewish people and would love to destroy them just as Hitler did.

The good news is God is not going to allow it. In spite of the Holocaust which came to an end in May 1945, the Jewish state of Israel was birthed some 36 months later in May of 1948. The devil thought he was going to get his way through Hitler, but God had a different plan. Not only did the war come to an end and a remnant of the Jewish people survive, but Israel became its own nation once again. It is mind-boggling to be alive in the same century that Israel has been formed into a nation once more. Israel has not been formally controlled by the Jewish people since the Babylonian exile in 597 BC, which was over 2,500 years ago. We are truly living in historic times.

When Balak realized the place he asked the prophet Balaam was not the right spot to curse Israel, he told him to move to another place in order to curse the Israeli camp. They set up another altar and make sacrifices. The third time Balaam goes to prophesy over Israel he does not even seek the Lord's counsel because he now knew it pleased the Lord to bless Israel. Suddenly the Spirit of God came upon him. He begins to bless Israel and finishes his prophecy by saying in Numbers 24:9 (NLT), "Like a lion, Israel crouches and lies down; like a lioness, who dares to arouse her? Blessed is everyone who blesses you, O Israel, and cursed is everyone who curses you." He then goes on to prophesy the defeat of Balak and his people, along with other cities in Canaan.

If Balaam were here today, he would be prophesying the same types of things. Likewise, God has put the same spirit that was on Balaam on you and me. This spirit is the Holy Spirit, the Spirit of God, that came over the prophet Balaam when he declared Israel's victories. He declared Israel would possess the land. Today we are seeing the same battle taking place in the Middle East. The conflict today is over which nation and people group Palestine belongs to. As Christians, we know who the land belongs to. The Bible outlines the boundaries of Israel very clearly. The Zionist movement (which is the movement that Jewish people from all over the world are returning to their homeland of Israel) we are witnessing is the Holy Spirit that is stirring in the Jewish people.

Not only is the Zionist movement a stirring in the Jewish people, but it is also a stirring in the heart of the Bride of Christ. The Church is Israel's most powerful ally today, as it should be. Any nation or people group who refuses Israel's right to the land will be put to shame. I believe one day before Jesus returns again, all of the land - every last inch of real estate - that belongs to the Jewish people according to God's Word will be under Israel's reign and jurisdiction. This does not mean foreigners cannot dwell in the land. It does not mean people of other religious beliefs cannot come visit. However, all of the land promised to Abraham and His literal Jewish descendants after him has been deeded by God to them as long as this planet is in existence.

The battle taking place in Israel right now is the battle for a strong Zionist government that honors Israel's right to exist as a Jewish and democratic state. If the Israeli government falls into the wrong hands, that is an Arab anti-Zionist political party, then the door is open to cutting off democracy and opening the door to something much worse like Sharia law. The time to step up and defend Israel as a believer in Christ is now. The time to join both ministries and political organizations that support Israel's right to exist is now. The Lord is counting on us, His glorious Church, to step up their game and defend His chosen nation!

It is also important as Christians that we pray for the salvation of the Jewish people. While many Jews have not yet come to know Jesus Christ as their personal Lord and Savior, there is a growing number of Jewish believers in Jesus in Israel today. As more and more Jewish people come to the knowledge of the truth, that Jesus is indeed the Son of God, I believe we are going to see global revival like this world has never seen before! If anyone can understand the richness of the sacred texts of the Scriptures, it is the Jewish believer.

The Apostle Paul explains what is going on spiritually with the Jewish people and their acceptance of Jesus as the Messiah. He tells the church at Corinth in 2 Corinthians 3:13-16 (NLT), "We are not like Moses, who put a veil over his face so the people of Israel would not see the glory, even though it was destined to fade away. But the people's minds were hardened, and to this day whenever the old covenant is being read, the same veil covers their [the Jewish people's] minds so they cannot understand the truth. And this veil can be removed only by believing in Christ. Yes, even today when they read Moses' writings, their hearts are covered with that veil, and they do not understand. But whenever someone turns to the Lord, the veil is taken away." Our prayer as the church should be: "Take away the veil Lord! Open the eyes of Your people Father!"

I believe one reason more Jewish people have not come to Christ yet is because the Church is not asking enough. If you are an intercessor, and we all are to some degree, then having the Jewish people on your prayer list is a must. If you are praying for revival and a global harvest, it is not going to happen unless both Gentiles AND Jews are coming to know Christ. Through Christ we are two separate people groups made into one. Most of your favorite Scriptures were spoken and/or written by Jewish people. I say this because as Christians it is important that we remember the Jewish heritage of our Christian faith.

This reminds me of the phrase "never forget where you came from". The phrase is often quoted when a person achieves some sort of success - like rising to the top in a business or achieving a big dream - as a reminder to that person to not forget where they started in life. All of us are in part a product of our upbringing. When we appreciate those who helped us flourish, like our parents, teachers, mentors, and friends, then we are giving respect and honor back to those who helped us along the way.

This expression "never forget where you came from" can also be applied to our Christian faith. If the Jewish people had not faithfully stewarded the oracles of God, there would be no Bible. Without the Jewish Jesus, there would be no Savior. Without the Jewish Apostle Paul, there would be no letters to the churches. Perhaps a more accurate expression "never forget where your Christian faith came from" is appropriate. Your faith came primarily through Jewish men and women of God. The gospel went to the Jewish people living in Israel first, then to the rest of the world. This is the way God ordained it.

This does not mean one people group is more valuable to God than the other. It means God chose to do this for His own divine purposes. His ways are much higher than our ways. The Lord knew before time began that He would create one big family of both Jews and Gentiles with the same firstborn birthright through Christ. The gospel began with the Jewish people and the summing up of all things in these last days will end with the Jewish people. You and I have the privilege as co-heirs with Christ to invite all people into the house of God. The Apostle Paul tells us in Romans 8:16-17 (NLT), "For His Spirit joins with our spirit to affirm that we are God's children. And since we are His children, we are His heirs. In fact, together with Christ we are heirs of God's glory. But if we are to share His glory, we must also share His suffering."

In these last days God has sent forth His Holy Spirit. The day of judgment is coming. Anyone who has not received Jesus Christ into their heart, whether they are Jewish or non-Jewish, will be cut off from the inheritance God meant for us to have. This is why we testify about God and what He has done for us. This is why we warn people that there is an afterlife, and there are only two destinations: Heaven or Hell. Both destinations go on forever and ever. We get to choose which place we are going to go to for eternity. The ones who receive the love of God and accept the forgiveness of sins that can only come through His Son Jesus will go on forever to be with God in Heaven. Those who reject Jesus as their Savior will go on forever in Hell, where there is eternal torment.

When Jesus walked the earth and ministered in Israel, there were many who believed and were saved from the wrath of God to come. However, there were also many who did not believe and became so offended at Jesus' message that they began to persecute Christ's followers after they were done putting Him to death. This same persecution of believers has carried on to this day. The world is not going to approve and accept God's message. 1 John 4:5-6 (NLT) tells us, "Those people belong to this world, so they speak from the world's viewpoint, and the world listens to them. But we belong to God, and those who know God listen to us. If they do not belong to God, they do not listen to us. That is how we know if someone has the Spirit of truth or the spirit of deception."

Brothers and sisters, the world is so confused about what is going on in the Middle East. Many people simply do not know what God has said about Israel and the land upon which it sits. If we are not teaching about God's covenant and promises then people could find themselves standing against God and what He wants to do in and through Israel today. The Spirit of truth and the spirit of deception will never get along. One is from the light, as God is the light. The other is from the darkness, and we know there is no truth in the devil or his darkness. Light and darkness cannot co-exist. Light always prevails over darkness. When the light comes on, darkness must flee in Jesus' name!

As we embrace what God is doing in the Middle East today through the Zionist movement, let us remember our salvation came from the Jews. Let us remember Jesus Christ was born Jewish. He was born under the Law of Moses from the Old Testament. He walked blamelessly, following all of the Old Testament ordinances. He did what no other human being possibly could. When this Jewish man was wrongfully persecuted and put to death, He had no sin. Because He had no sin, death had no hold on His body. On the third day after His death, Jesus rose from the dead. He proved Himself 100% faithful, even physically revisiting the disciples before ascending back into Heaven where He is still alive today!

You and I partake of this Spirit that rose Jesus Christ from the grave. This Spirit was first released in an upper room of Jerusalem during the Feast of Weeks (also called Shavuot, or Pentecost). The land of Israel is a physical testament as to where Jesus walked, taught, and brought salvation to the whole world. It is the place God chose to make His name great. Let us celebrate what God is doing in Israel today. Let us declare like the prophet Ezekiel in Ezekiel 11:17 (NIV), "This is what the Sovereign LORD says: I will gather you from the nations and bring you back from the countries where you have been scattered, and I will give you back the land of Israel again." Biblical prophecy is unfolding before our eyes. The Jewish people are coming home. May we as the global church be the welcome committee that stands for, celebrates, and even defends their God-given right to do so.

REASON TWO

Romans Eleven

One of the primary arguments I hear from people who profess to be Christians but do not support the Jewish people's right to return to their homeland in Israel is that Israel is an Old Testament thing. They argue that Israel is now just a "spiritual" Israel and that the Church is the new Israel (see Romans 9:6). While there is truth in this statement in that all must accept Jesus Christ in order to inherit eternal salvation, whether they are a literal descendant of Abraham (making them genetically Jewish) or a Gentile (non-Jewish), the statement is not accurate when it pertains to the land of Israel we see today. Because of God's promise to Abraham, the land of Israel always has and always will belong to the Jewish people.

However, just like Gentiles must accept Jesus Christ to go to Heaven, so Jewish people must accept Jesus as the Messiah to go to Heaven as well. There is no free pass into Heaven. All people must come to repentance and receive the free gift of Christ's salvation. The Apostle Paul explains in Romans 2:6-11 (NIV), "God 'will repay each person according to what they have done.' To those who by persistence in doing good seek glory, honor and immortality, He will give eternal life. But for those who are self-seeking and who reject the truth and follow evil, there will be wrath and anger. There will be trouble and distress for every human being who does evil: first for the Jew, then for the Gentile; but glory, honor and peace for everyone who does good: first for the Jew, then for the Gentile. For God does not show favoritism."

It is important to note that God does not love one people group more than another. The Lord's covenant with Israel was by God's divine choice. Isaiah 49:6 (NLT) says concerning the Messiah, "You will do more than restore the people of Israel to Me. I will make You a light to the Gentiles, and You will bring My salvation to the ends of the earth." The whole purpose of Jesus' ministry was to restore everyone, Jews and Gentiles, back to God the Father through His own blood. God's will is that all people would know Him, not just the Hebrew people. In the New Testament, the Apostle Paul explains that because the Jewish people in large part rejected Jesus as the Messiah, God has caused salvation to go to all the nations instead.

The Apostle Paul tells us in Romans 10:1-4 (NIV), "Brothers and sisters, my heart's desire and prayer to God for the Israelites is that they may be saved. For I can testify about them that they are zealous for God, but their zeal is not based on knowledge. Since they did not know the righteousness of God and sought to establish their own, they did not submit to God's righteousness. Christ is the culmination of the Law so that there may be righteousness for everyone who believes." The Israelites became so zealous for the Law of God that they stumbled right past its purpose. They missed the good news that righteousness is obtained by faith in the Messiah and not by works of the Law.

Righteousness cannot be earned. It is freely given to all who believe in Jesus' name. The works prove the faith (James 2:17). However, works of man cannot establish righteousness with God. The message of true righteousness through faith in Christ offended the Jews at the time of Christ and during Paul's ministry. Romans 10:16 tells us that not all of Israel accepted the good news of Christ's salvation when He came. We are living in a fascinating period of time in history. Today more and more Jews are coming to know Jesus Christ as the resurrected Messiah. Messianic Jewish congregations are now all over the world and growing.

Some of God's promises found in chapter 11 of the book of Romans should excite the Church, as we pray God restores the nation of Israel and brings the Hebrew people to the knowledge of Jesus as their one true Messiah. For over a millennia, the church at large has written off the Jewish people as rejected by God. Somehow it was just accepted that the Jewish people were scattered abroad for their rejection of Christ, and that's the way it has been for hundreds of years - and maybe even should be. However, to the Biblically astute, Romans 11 has waved its hand for centuries that God is nowhere near finished with Israel.

Romans 11:1-2 (NASB95) tells us, "I say then, God has not rejected His people, has He? May it never be! For I too am an Israelite, a descendant of Abraham, of the tribe of Benjamin. God has not cast away His people whom He foreknew." Just because Israel forsook the Son of God when He came does not mean God forever turned His back on Israel and the promises He has made to them. The New Testament has by no means made the promises of God in the Old Testament null and void, as some within the church have erroneously assumed.

The promises we find all the way in Genesis can still be found in the world we are living in today. Have you ever seen a rainbow after a heavy rainfall? Did you know that the rainbow was put there by God as a covenant with mankind to never flood the earth again? Furthermore, this covenant God made with mankind and every living creature was recorded on a Jewish scroll in the Law of Moses. The Torah recounts this permanent covenant in Genesis 9:8-17. In our Bibles, the Old Testament comes first. Likewise, the Jewish people came first. Whether we understand why God chose the Hebrews first or not, He did so. He is God, and His ways are much higher than ours.

Today God has left a remnant of Jewish people on the earth who believe in Jesus. The Apostle Paul makes a comparison between what has happened among the Jewish people during his day and what happened in the days of Elijah the prophet. Paul says in Romans 11:2-5 (NASB95), "Or do you not know what the Scripture says in the passage about Elijah, how he pleads with God against Israel? 'Lord, they have killed Your prophets, they have torn down Your altars, and I alone am left, and they are seeking my life.' But what is the divine response to him? 'I have kept for Myself seven thousand men who have not bowed the knee to Baal.' In the same way then, there has also come to be at the present time a remnant according to God's gracious choice."

When the Apostle Paul wrote this his biggest opponents were the Jewish leaders. I'm sure he felt a whole lot like the prophet Elijah, who lived in strong opposition with Ahab and Jezebel, having to flee for his own life. Likewise, maybe you feel a little bit like Paul and Elijah. If you are surrounded by unbelievers and people who are not seeking God at work or school, you might find yourself swimming upstream. While everyone else is going along with the world - partying, living loosely, and doing whatever they want - you are attending church, listening to Christian music, and staying sober.

The Lord tells us we are going to be at odds with the rest of the world. This friction is what causes us to shine. Philippians 2:14-15 (NLT) instructs us, "Do everything without complaining and arguing, so that no one can criticize you. Live clean, innocent lives as children of God, shining like bright lights in a world full of crooked and perverse people." While none of us are perfect, following God is going to cause you to stand out in the midst of the world when you do your best to honor Him. The Lord's will is that all people would come to know Him, and one way He reaches the lost is through you. He will use your life as a testament to His goodness and mercy.

We are living in an era of grace. If it were not for God's grace, you and I would have no hope for salvation. God's grace is freely given. It is not based upon merit or good works. You cannot earn the right to go to Heaven. It is based upon God's kindness and upon Him willfully choosing us. The Apostle Paul writes in Romans 11:6 (NIV), "And if by grace, then it cannot be based on works; if it were, grace would no longer be grace." The Lord has chosen a remnant among the Jewish people today who can see clearly that Jesus is the promised Messiah. While we pray that all Jewish people would see Jesus Christ as their Messiah, the Lord has allowed their hearts to be hardened and their eyes blinded to the truth.

Romans 11:7-10 (NIV) goes on to say, "What then? What the people of

Israel sought so earnestly they did not obtain. The elect among them did, but the others were hardened, as it is written: 'God gave them a spirit of stupor, eyes that could not see and ears that could not hear, to this very day.' (Deuteronomy 29:4) And David says: 'May their table become a snare and a trap, a stumbling block and a retribution for them. May their eyes be darkened so they cannot see, and their backs be bent forever.'" (Psalm 69:22-23) After reading this passage of Scripture it might be tempting to say the Jewish people got what they deserved. They continually rebelled against God's commandments, served false gods, and ultimately rejected the Son of God.

However, God never forgot His covenant with David, nor His covenant with Abraham, Isaac, or Jacob. The Lord never retracted His promise to be Israel's redeemer. The Israelites stumbled but not beyond what God can repair. The Lord has always had a fiery passion for the Jewish people. He loves the Hebrew people deeply, as a groom is madly in love with his bride. As such, He requires wholehearted devotion. God tells His people in Exodus 34:14 (NASB95), "For you shall not worship any other god, for the LORD, whose name is Jealous, is a jealous God." The fact that God is jealous for His people is a rather flattering thought. The same is true today. God is jealous for His church.

Hebrews 12:29 tells us God is a consuming fire. He wants to consume the hearts of His people! The Apostle Paul says in Romans 11:11 (ESV), "So I ask, did Israel stumble in order that they might fall? By no means! Rather, through their trespass salvation has come to the Gentiles, so as to make Israel jealous." Israel has not fallen, as some nation of a past civilization. On the contrary, they have stumbled, and a remnant has been saved.

The ongoing love affair between the nation of Israel and Almighty God continues to this day. The Lord has always had a jealous love for Israel since He made His covenant with Abraham. Today, God is still jealous with love for the Jewish state.

Because Israel rejected the Son of God, the Lord has allowed them to be provoked to jealousy by turning His salvation to the Gentile nations, just as they provoked Him to jealousy when they served Baal's and other false gods. It's a fascinating and profound relationship God has with the Jewish people. As the psalmist declares in admiration in Psalm 92:5 (ESV), "How great are your works, O LORD! Your thoughts are very deep!" The Lord already knew Israel would break its covenant with Him. He already knew Israel's rejection of the Messiah would happen long before Jesus' birth. In His great knowledge and infinite foresight, the Lord allowed the rejection in order to display His glory to the ends of the earth! Now all nations have and are still coming to know Jesus Christ as the King of all kings and the Lord of all lords. It is important to understand why Paul wrote that God turned to the Gentiles in order to make Paul's kinsmen jealous. When Paul preached, his biggest opponents were jealous Jewish men. Acts 13:45 (NASB95) explains, "But when the Jews saw the crowds, they were filled with jealousy and began contradicting the things spoken by Paul, and were blaspheming." The Jewish leaders were super jealous of Paul and his flourishing ministry. Paul was drawing large crowds, likely much larger crowds than the Jewish leaders when they taught.

The Scriptures go on to say in Acts 13:46-47 (NIV), "Then Paul and Barnabas answered them boldly: 'We had to speak the word of God to you first. Since you reject it and do not consider yourselves worthy of eternal life, we now turn to the Gentiles. For this is what the Lord has commanded us: 'I have made you a light for the Gentiles, that you may bring salvation to the ends of the earth.' (Isaiah 49:6)" We see here a principle of humility. One reason the Jewish leaders rejected the gospel message is because of their pride. These religious leaders had become so bound up in their own traditions that they missed what the Lord was doing. Their own pride caused them to stumble. King Solomon warns us in Proverbs 16:18 (ESV) saying, "Pride goes before destruction, and a haughty spirit before a fall."

The good news today is Israel's downfall some 2,000 years ago is not permanent. The day of restoration is coming, and we are seeing it before our very eyes! God's mercies run from generation to generation. He has not forgotten His covenant with the Jewish people. The Apostle Paul knew God was not forever done with the Jewish people, even when he was likely very frustrated with the synagogue leaders. He tells the Church in Romans 11:12 (NASB95), "Now if their transgression is riches for the world and their failure is riches for the Gentiles, how much more will their fulfillment be!" The spiritual and physical riches that came with the good news that Jesus Christ came to redeem us transformed the entire earth.

Because of Jesus, people are breaking out of generational curses. Because of Jesus, people are breaking bad habits, casting aside wrong thinking, and stepping into their gifts and callings of God. The amount of good, both spiritually and physically, that has come from the gospel and the teaching of God's principles for success in life have revolutionized the world. Romans 11:12 is another promise of God that we should be declaring and calling for today. When the Jewish people come to know the true gospel, that Jesus is the Son of God, the Apostle Paul says the world will see riches and blessings like never before!

This is why you should make it a personal endeavor to be a blessing to the nation of Israel. If you want to fulfill your calling and experience more favor and blessing, start by praying for Israel. Israel's redemption is a heavyweight blessing for the entire world. That's why the devil hates Israel. He hates the Holy Land and what God is doing. The good news is it doesn't matter what our enemy thinks. We have God! He says no weapon formed against us will succeed. He says we are the head and not the tail. He says whatever we put our hands to will prosper. When you lock into the promises of God, strongholds of the enemy are going to break.

Every time I sit down to write about Israel, even if it's only for 5 or 10 minutes, I can feel the anointing of the Holy Spirit in a greater measure throughout the rest of the day. The primary modern-day issue impacting the entire world is Israel. Israel is constantly under attack. Her enemies are launching missiles at her throughout the year. They probably do not realize it, but they are being used by Satan to try to bring her down. As Christians, it is our duty to pray for the safety and wellbeing of this chosen nation. Proverbs 11:25 (NIV) tells us, "A generous person will prosper; whoever refreshes others will be refreshed." When we pray for Israel, God not only blesses Israel, but He causes those blessings to come right back on us as well.

Paul goes on to say in Romans 11:13 (NKJV), "For I speak to you Gentiles; inasmuch as I am an apostle to the Gentiles, I magnify my ministry." The Apostle Paul was confident in His call to minister to the Gentile nations. He did not allow his own countrymen to cause him to waver. He went against the grain. He went to the Gentiles, who were previously excluded from Israel and the promises God had made to them. Paul tells the Church in Ephesians 2:14 (NLT), "For Christ Himself has brought peace to us. He united Jews and Gentiles into one people when, in His own body on the cross, He broke down the wall of hostility that separated us."

Before Jesus came there was a "wall of hostility" between Israel and the rest of the world. This wall still exists for those who have not come to know Christ yet. That's why there is so much hostility towards Israel today. If you are not in Christ, then you are in darkness as to what God is doing in Israel. Those who know the Word know that it is wrong to curse Israel, for those who curse her will be cursed by God Most High. When Paul's own countrymen refused to believe the gospel message, Paul tells them in Romans 11:14 (NLT), "For I want somehow to make the people of Israel jealous of what you Gentiles have, so I might save some of them." It is a very interesting statement Paul makes about intentionally trying to provoke his own people to jealousy for the sake of the gospel. The Apostle Paul knew the Messiah had come into the world, and the ones the Messiah came to first missed it!

The good news Jesus came to offer the world is freedom. Paul's desire was for his Jewish brothers and sisters to see the spiritual freedom the Gentiles had and for them to desire that freedom. The same is true today. God wants people to see Christ in you and to desire to have what you have. When we get our eyes focused on Christ and on His kingdom, there is going to be something different about us. Others should want what we have. The Lord has called us to be different. Titus 2:14 (KJV) says, "Who gave Himself for us, that He might redeem us from all iniquity, and purify unto Himself a peculiar people, zealous of good works."

The Lord has called you to be peculiar. You are unique and one of a kind. There is no one like you. Your identity in Christ is what defines you. Because you have His Spirit in you, you are being transformed from the inside out. You are being made into who God wants you to be, as you submit to Him and to His Word. Before Christ came, God chose to set apart the Hebrew people as a forerunner of what was coming. The Apostle Paul says in Galatians 3:22-24 (NIV), "But Scripture has locked up everything under the control of sin, so that what was promised, being given through faith in Jesus Christ, might be given to those who believe. Before the coming of this faith, we were held in custody under the Law, locked up until the faith that was to come would be revealed. So the Law was our guardian until Christ came that we might be justified by faith."

Another translation of the Scriptures say that the Law was our "tutor" that leads us to Christ. The point Paul is making is the Law is based on works and cannot justify people, because everyone sins. The only way to get out from under the control of sin is by faith in Jesus Christ. God chose the Hebrews to give and uphold the Law until Jesus came to fulfill it. Because of this, the Hebrews are the original olive tree. They are by natural birth the children of Abraham. Romans 11:15-16 (NLT) tells us, "For since their rejection meant that God offered salvation to the rest of the world, their acceptance will be even more wonderful. It will be life for those who were dead! And since Abraham and the other patriarchs were holy, their descendants will also be holy—just as the entire batch of dough is holy because the portion given as an offering is holy. For if the roots of the tree are holy, the branches will be, too."

There is a holy inheritance for those who walk in faith like Abraham and the other patriarchs of the Bible. For the Jewish people, they are in the literal bloodline of Abraham, Isaac, and Jacob. For the Gentile people, we have been grafted in by walking in faith like Abraham. Paul emphasizes the original covenant God made with the people of Israel when he admonishes the church for any arrogance they have towards the Jews. He says in Romans 11:17-18 (NASB95), "But if some of the branches were broken off, and you, being a wild olive, were grafted in among them and became partaker with them of the rich root of the olive tree, do not be arrogant toward the branches; but if you are arrogant, remember that it is not you who supports the root, but the root supports you."

The root of the Christian faith comes from the Jewish people. There is a false teaching that is shot down by the Apostle Paul here. This false teaching is called replacement theology. Replacement theology (or supersessionism) is the belief that the Church has replaced Israel in God's plan. It teaches that the Jews are no longer God's people and that God no longer has a plan for Israel's future. Brothers and sisters, this is a grave error! Romans 11:17-18 warn us not to become so arrogant. Israel is the original olive tree. Gentiles are, by nature, a wild olive tree. Our Jewish roots support us. The branches do not support the root. Arrogance and misunderstanding is what has led churches to include supersessionism into their doctrine.

The devil would love for the Church to believe that God is done with the literal descendants of Abraham, Isaac, and Jacob. Adolf Hitler was one of his greatest champions in carrying out the atrocious Holocaust. Throughout the ages the devil has used others to try and destroy the

Jewish people. Why? Israel is the chosen people of God. As the Church, we have been grafted into the native olive tree. The One we follow and serve, Jesus the Messiah, is Jewish. How then can we cast aside the Jewish people knowing everything we believe stems from and came through the Jews?

The good news today is one day all of Israel will indeed be saved. The Apostle Paul continues to admonish and warn the church, when he goes on to say in Romans 11:19-21 (NASB95), "You will say then, 'Branches were broken off so that I might be grafted in.' Quite right, they were broken off for their unbelief, but you stand by your faith. Do not be conceited, but fear; for if God did not spare the natural branches, He will not spare you, either." The number one way to be cut off from God is unbelief. If God temporarily cut off a portion of His own Jewish people for rejecting His gospel message through His Son Jesus Christ, then He certainly will cut off those who are not of the Jewish people that are in unbelief also.

God does not show favoritism or partiality. He is love, and He is just. All people, Jews and Gentiles alike, have the opportunity to receive the free gift of Christ's salvation. The suffering, the pain, and the rejection the King of the entire universe went through is not taken lightly by God in Heaven. When people reject God's greatest gift to mankind ever, it is an insult. Rejection and unbelief of what God has said will ultimately result in separation from God for eternity. The reality of hell as an eternal place is just as true as the reality of Heaven being an eternal place. While we don't like to talk about hell and how horrific it is, that does not negate the Biblical truth that there is a hell and many people are going there.

Recently I saw in the news a renown worship leader who decided to renounce his faith publicly because he could not believe that if God was all-loving that He would send people to hell. The same Jesus Who came to offer redemption to all who put their faith in Him for salvation, is the same Jesus who tells us in detail about hell. Jesus tells us in Matthew 25:41-43 (NLT), "Then the King will turn to those on the left and say, 'Away with you, you cursed ones, into the eternal fire prepared for the devil and his demons. For I was hungry, and you didn't feed Me. I was thirsty, and you didn't give Me a drink. I was a stranger, and you didn't invite Me into your home. I was naked, and you didn't give Me clothing. I was sick and in prison, and you didn't visit Me." It is unfortunate that this worship minister turned his back on the faith, as it hurt a lot of people who looked up to him, but the truth is he was being deceived by the enemy into a state of unbelief.

Another misconception I have heard people who are pro-Israel but have run past the mark, so to speak, say is that if you are born Jewish then you automatically go to Heaven, even if you haven't received Jesus as your personal Lord and Savior. This also is unbiblical. The Bible makes it explicitly clear that both Jews and Gentiles must come to Christ for salvation. There are no free passes to Heaven. All must come to repentance and receive the free gift of Christ's salvation. As aforementioned, Romans 2:9-11 (NIV) says, "There will be trouble and distress for every human being who does evil: first for the Jew, then for the Gentile; but glory, honor and peace for everyone who does good: first for the Jew, then for the Gentile. For God does not show favoritism."

There is an interesting principle throughout Scripture of God dealing with the Jews first and then the Gentiles. The Jews, as Paul puts it, are the original olive tree. The Gentiles are the wild olive tree. Romans 11:22 (NASB95) tells us, "Behold then the kindness and severity of God; to those who fell, severity, but to you, God's kindness, if you continue in His kindness; otherwise you also will be cut off." If you think about two siblings, like an older brother and a younger brother, the older brother is usually held more responsible growing up by nature. The older brother was born first and knows right from wrong before the younger brother. However, as both brothers grow older and become men they are treated equally.

The same thing is true with Jews and Gentiles. The Jewish people were taught the Law of God first. Jesus went first to the Jewish people to share the good news of God's grace. Then when Pentecost came, the Church was born. Now the "younger brother", or the Church, has joined "older brother" in both the responsibilities and privileges of stewarding the things of God. So my question is, is the older brother more valuable to his parents or is the younger brother? The answer, of course, is neither. They are both deeply and equally loved by their parents. It's the same way with God.

God loves both Jews and non-Jews equally. Jews came first, just like the older sibling comes first after being born. While this analogy is not perfect, it does drive home the point that God is not partial to one people group or the other. As the "younger brother", which is the Church, has had the awesome privilege of watching Israel, or it's older brother, be restored in these last days, we as the family of God should rejoice! We should celebrate what God is doing in the Holy Land today. Likewise, whenever someone attacks "big brother", we should be defensive and passionate to defend him.

God is the Good Father. He is going to deal with both of his children, which is the Church and Israel. He is going to prune us. He is going to cut off those who are not truly His. God has given all of us a choice. I believe in these last days we are living in, God is drawing a line in the sand. Either you will follow Him, even if it means being persecuted, or you will turn the other way and follow the world. It is important to note that God extends kindness to all who come to Him. Psalm 103:8 (NASB95) tells us, "The LORD is compassionate and gracious, slow to anger and abounding in lovingkindness." When the Scriptures say that God "cut off" people, it is not because it is unwarranted or because God did not give His people a second chance (or a third, fourth, fifth, etc).

The Bible makes it clear that God is very patient until His time of mercy is over. Paul explains in Romans 10:19-21 (NLT), "But I ask, did the people of Israel really understand (the gospel)? Yes, they did, for even in the time of Moses, God said, 'I will rouse your jealousy through people who are not even a nation. I will provoke your anger through the foolish Gentiles.' And later Isaiah spoke boldly for God, saying, 'I was found by people who were not looking for Me. I showed Myself to those who were not asking for Me.' But regarding Israel, God said, 'All day long I opened My arms to them, but they were disobedient and rebellious.'"

The good news today is God's mercy is still available to you and me. Anyone who still has air in their lungs and a heartbeat is not outside the mercy of God. The Lord's arms are still stretched out to all people. The Lord's will was never to cut off Israel from the new covenant. His will was that Israel would recognize the Messiah when He came, but because of their hardened hearts they missed it. However, God is not finished with the Jewish people. On the contrary, He is more than able to bring them back into the house. The Apostle Paul continues, saying in Romans 11:23-24 (NKJV), "And they also, if they do not continue in unbelief, will be grafted in, for God is able to graft them in again. For if you were cut out of the olive tree which is wild by nature, and were grafted contrary to nature into a cultivated olive tree, how much more will these, who are natural branches, be grafted into their own olive tree?"

The Hebrew people are of the cultivated olive tree. The Gentiles are from the olive tree of the wilderness. The heritage of the Jewish people runs much further back than even the oldest church in existence today. You may have heard the idiom "it's in the blood". The things of God are already built into the Jews' personality and character. For example, you may know of a family that is all athletes. Dad was a terrific athlete. Mom was a great athlete. Now their children and grandchildren are really athletic. It's in the blood. In the same way, the Hebrews have thousands of years of the oracles of God running through their blood. This is what Paul is talking about. They are of the original assembly of God we read about in the Old Testament.

Knowing this should make the Church humble towards Israel. The Apostle Paul warns us to not be arrogant about possessing the new covenant of grace that much of Israel has missed. Israel is precious in the eyes of God and should be precious in the eyes of the Church. They are the tribe, or family, we have been grafted into. It is important we understand what is going on with Israel and the Jewish people right now. Romans 11:25 (NASB95) tells us, "For I do not want you, brethren, to be uninformed of this mystery-- so that you will not be wise in your own estimation-- that a partial hardening has happened to Israel until the fullness of the Gentiles has come in." Seeing God reserve a remnant of Israel is not a new thing. As we read the Scriptures, more than once God tells His prophets that He was saving a remnant of Israel that would be faithful to Him and that He would preserve them for the sake of His covenant with their ancestors.

Leading up to and during the exile of Israel and Judah, the prophet Isaiah declared many things concerning what was to come. The prophet declares in Isaiah 10:21-22 (NASB95), "A remnant will return, the remnant of Jacob, to the mighty God. For though your people, O Israel, may be like the sand of the sea, only a remnant within them will return; a destruction is determined, overflowing with righteousness." When the Jewish people were exiled from the land of Israel during the Old Testament times, the stage was being set for the coming Messiah to enter. Isaiah goes on to prophesy in Isaiah 11:1 (ESV), "There shall come forth a shoot from the stump of Jesse, and a branch from his roots shall bear fruit."

Jesus Christ is the shoot that has come forth from Jesse. Jesus is the branch of eternal redemption that has come forth from the cultivated olive tree. If you are Gentile, you have been grafted into the Jewish olive tree. If you are Jewish, you have been grafted back into your own tree through Christ's sacrifice. The commonality Jews and Gentiles have is the need to be redeemed and to be grafted back into a right relationship with God the Father. The only redeemer there is is Jesus Christ! Only the blood of Jesus can permanently wash away our sins. Jesus prophesied that He would merge both people groups, Jews and Gentiles, into one. He tells us in John 10:16 (NLT), "I have other sheep, too, that are not in this sheepfold. I must bring them also. They will listen to my voice, and there will be one flock with one shepherd."

The merging of two people groups, Jews and Gentiles, was inevitable - even from the beginning. God has always had a plan to redeem the entire world and restore mankind to Himself. He never lost control because His children got so far out of line that He could not save anymore. The truth is God has given all people freewill. We get to choose what we believe, who we believe, and if we are going to serve God. The Lord is not going to force us to believe the truth that He has told us. However, there is a consequence either way. For those who believe and are obedient, there is reward. For those who disbelieve and go their own way, there is punishment.

When Jesus explains that He is the Good Shepherd, His Jewish audience was already being divided over what He said. John 10:19 (NASB95) says, "A division occurred again among the Jews because of these words." It is important to note that not everyone is going to agree with what Jesus has said. The words of Christ were divisive in His day, and they are still divisive today. The good news is I believe you and I are believers. We know our Redeemer lives! The Lord is merciful, and His hands are still stretched out to anyone who will come to Him. The partial hardening we see in Israel towards Jesus as the Messiah is not forever. The day of their eyes being opened is drawing near.

The Apostle Paul tells us in Romans 11:26-27 (NLT), "And so all Israel will be saved. As the Scriptures say, 'The One who rescues will come from Jerusalem, and He will turn Israel away from ungodliness. And this is My covenant with them, that I will take away their sins.'" Jesus Christ is the One who comes from Zion, or Jerusalem, to take away sin and remove ungodliness. As John the Baptist declares in John 1:29 (NASB95), "Behold, the Lamb of God who takes away the sin of the world!" It is important to note that John the Baptist did not say Jesus only takes away the sin of Israel. Jesus takes away the sin of every nation and every type of person in the world who comes to Him.

One of the biggest opponents of early Christianity was the Jewish religious leaders. The Apostle Paul, before he was converted and went by the name Saul, was one of them. Jesus' message of salvation, of being the Son of God, and of being redeemed out from under the Law was considered blasphemy by the Jewish leaders during that time. When the Apostle Paul was writing the Christians at Rome, he was writing as someone who had the memory of once being a persecutor. He knew how much the Jews hated the gospel message and anyone who believed in it, because at one time he was one of them. After Paul's conversion (see Acts 9:1-19), Paul had the benefit of a strong knowledge of the Law and the Prophets (our Old Testament) and also the divine revelation of Jesus Christ. Paul had a gift of connecting the things of the Old Testament to what is now the New Testament.

He tells the believers at Rome in Romans 11:28 (NLT), "Many of the people of Israel are now enemies of the Good News, and this benefits you Gentiles. Yet they are still the people He loves because He chose their ancestors Abraham, Isaac, and Jacob." One of the common mistakes made by Christians is the belief that God is done with the Jewish people. The thought process is they rejected the Messiah so God just abandoned them and went to the rest of the world indefinitely. While it is true that many Jewish people are still unbelievers in terms of acknowledging Jesus as the Son of God, God certainly has not abandoned nor forgotten about them!

God's covenant that He made with Abraham, Isaac, and Jacob still stands. The Lord loved the patriarchs, and the blessing He put on them and their descendants is still active today.

The next verse, Romans 11:29, is one of my favorites of the entire Bible. It is one that speaks of God's divine call on Israel, but also applies to each of us individually. Romans 11:29 (ESV) says, "For the gifts and the calling of God are irrevocable." Brothers and sisters, God will never ever reverse or change His mind once He has called you and blessed you. No matter what you have been through or what you have done, the gifts God has given you and the call on your life cannot be revoked or forfeited. There is no mistake that is beyond the mercy and redemptive power of Almighty God. When the Apostle Paul tells us God's plans are irrevocable, it means they cannot be undone. Maybe today you feel unqualified, like you don't measure up. The good news is God does not call the qualified. He calls the unqualified. He calls people like Jacob, who was a deceiver, and Rahab, who was a prostitute.

He calls people like Paul, who once had Christians locked up and even killed, in order to testify about His goodness. The same truth applies to Israel. While Israel did reject the Messiah, God has not given up on them. The promises God made to Israel still stand. The promises God has made to you still stand. Because Jesus still lives we all can have hope for better days ahead. The plans of God are far beyond our understanding. Isaiah 55:8-9 (NIV) says, "'For My thoughts are not your thoughts, neither are your ways My ways,' declares the LORD. 'As the heavens are higher than the earth, so are My ways higher than your ways and My thoughts than your thoughts.'" The divine redemptive plan God has set into motion is one that we cannot understand except in part by what He shows us in His Word and by His Spirit. Even then, no man can possibly understand it all. Only God knows.

When times are hard, you can trust God. You can trust that He is always good and that He is working behind the scenes causing everything to fall into place. God has not forgotten about any people group on the earth. He is still calling Jews and Gentiles into His Kingdom. We just get to participate and co-labor with Him in doing so! The Apostle Paul goes on to say in Romans 11:30-31 (NCV), "At one time you refused to obey God. But now you have received mercy, because those people refused to obey. And now the Jews refuse to obey, because God showed mercy to you. But this happened so that they also can receive mercy from Him." The common theme here is all people, even Israel, have fallen into disobedience before God.

Whenever the Lord does something, He does it for His glory. Now that we know who God is by His Word, that He created all things and that He loves us, we should live our lives in a way that honors Him. He has shown mercy on us, even at a time when we were far away from Him. If you have been a believer for a long time, it might seem a little strange to consider yourself an enemy of God at one time. The truth is we all were. Romans 5:8-10 (NIV) tells us, "But God demonstrates His own love for us in this: While we were still sinners, Christ died for us. Since we have now been justified by His blood, how much more shall we be saved from God's wrath through Him! For if, while we were God's enemies, we were reconciled to Him through the death of His Son, how much more, having been reconciled, shall we be saved through His life!"

In Christ, you have gone from enemy to friend. You have gone from sinner to saved. You have gone from wrath to mercy. Our sinful nature is actually hostile towards God and His ways. The good news is God has sent a Deliverer, One who walked as the Son of God in the flesh and gave up His life to set us free. This man, Jesus Christ, is an Israelite by birth. He rose from the grave, because He had no sin. Because He had no sin - and the consequences of sin is death (see Romans 6:23) - His body literally rose from the grave. His body never decayed like the rest of the dead (Psalm 16:10). This body of Christ is a testament to the power Jesus possesses. If God can raise His Son from the dead, then in His Son's name He can raise us from the dead to be with Him forever!

From the beginning God had a plan to redeem everyone from the curse of sin and death. Romans 11:32 (NASB95) says, "For God has shut up all in disobedience so that He may show mercy to all." God chose to bring salvation to the world through His Son. Anyone seeking to earn the righteousness of God is going to fail. Righteousness can only come by faith, or believing, in Jesus. No amount of good works, or even attending church, can save you. The notion that all paths lead to Heaven is also a lie. There is only one path, and God has made it clear to the world what that path is. Only those who believe will find it and inherit eternal life.

I've heard people say not to harm any other living thing or to do good - that is, if my good deeds outweigh my bad deeds - then I'll go to Heaven. While this all may seem rational and good to the human mind, it still does not change our standing with God. The Apostle Paul tells us in Romans 3:9-12 (ESV), "What then? Are we Jews any better off? No, not at all. For we have already charged that all, both Jews and Greeks, are under sin, as it is written: 'None is righteous, no, not one; no one understands; no one seeks for God. All have turned aside; together they have become worthless; no one does good, not even one.' (Psalm 14:1-3)" Here Paul is quoting a psalm of King David.

The reality is apart from Jesus Christ we are all useless. Our value, our worth, and who we are all stems from our identity in Jesus. If you don't know Jesus, you don't know who you are meant to be. Jesus is the standard and the example we are to follow. Throughout my own life I have struggled with this. I've always been a goal-oriented and success-driven individual. I have known the Lord from a very young age. Nonetheless, when I'm not careful, I begin to stumble into the wrong thinking that my value in life comes from what I do and how successful I am by the world's standards. While I am a huge advocate for people pursuing their dreams and accomplishing great things, none of these activities or pursuits are what give us value in the eyes of God.

If you do great things, carry a full-time job, and raise your children successfully, you are no more or less valuable to God than someone who has struggled their whole life, could never hold down a job, and failed to give their children what they needed. There are people who have run Fortune 500 companies that are doing things that are an abomination to God. Then there are people who've gotten a divorce and struggled with an addiction their whole life that are more righteous than the successful CEO. The Lord looks at the heart. What He sees as valuable is not what we see. This is why we need to keep our eyes on Christ above and not on the things of this world.

The Lord can see far beyond anything our minds or hearts can fathom. He has always existed, unlike us. The Apostle Paul exclaims in Romans 11:33 (NASB95), "Oh, the depth of the riches both of the wisdom and knowledge of God! How unsearchable are His judgments and unfathomable His ways!" When you consider the universe and the vastness thereof, consider how great our God is Who created all that it contains. The sun sits perfectly at the center of the solar system, while the earth and other planets orbit it just perfectly as He has willed them to. The atmosphere of earth is designed just right so we can breathe the air and enjoy the sunlight during the day and the stars at night. Right now we are literally standing on a planet that is spinning around and around. Gravity holds us in place. That planet is orbiting the sun at just the right angles, causing the four seasons of the year. The endless and vast design of the universe declares the glory of God!

Job 9:10 (NKJV) says, "He does great things past finding out, Yes, wonders without number." Even with as much knowledge and information as we now have, we are still far from knowing just how great and glorious God truly is. When nothing seems right in the world, we can always find rest knowing the Lord is still on His throne. Our eternal resting place with Him awaits us after this life. The Lord is still doing wonders without number. When you pray, pray with boldness and confidence. The same Jesus who turned water into wine, walked on water, healed all who were sick, and raised people from the dead is the same Jesus who is listening when you pray.

Ask big. Pray bold prayers. The Lord wants to do great things in your life, but you have to ask Him. He does not need the approval of a doctor before

He heals someone. He does not need the bank to underwrite the loan so you will have the funds needed. He can use a doctor or a banker, but He is God. He did not consult the experts when He designed the universe. He did not ask the surgeon how to build the heart or the brain when He created the baby in the mother's womb. As Romans 11:34 (NLT) says, "For who can know the LORD's thoughts? Who knows enough to give Him advice?" Friend, no one knows more than our God. No one can get it done like Him.

Concerning the nation of Israel, for those who love her it can be overwhelming to look at the Middle East and think, "What a mess! There is so much violence and war." However, God is God, and He sees everything that is happening around Israel today. He is the One who has brought this vibrant country back to life and has drawn many of the Jewish people back home. No expert or politician could ever single-handedly have caused this, not without the Lord leading him or her to do so. Israel is a testament to the Scriptures, where much of what we read about and study in the Bible has taken place. Tours of different landmarks, sites, and places where Jesus walked abound in the Holy Land.

One reason I believe the Lord has revived Israel in these last days is so that all the world will see that everything He has said in His Word is true. He is making the truth more loud and clear than ever. Hebrews 12:24-25 (NLT) warns us, "You have come to Jesus, the One who mediates the new covenant between God and people, and to the sprinkled blood, which speaks of forgiveness instead of crying out for vengeance like the blood of Abel. Be careful that you do not refuse to listen to the One who is speaking. For if the people of Israel did not escape when they refused to listen to Moses, the earthly messenger, we will certainly not escape if we reject the One who speaks to us from Heaven!"

God has given us the free gift of eternal life in His Son Jesus. Jesus and His eternal words still speak today. The Lord is warning us from Heaven that those who refuse to accept Jesus will come under judgment and condemnation. Jesus Christ is the only way to be forgiven and redeemed. The Lord does not owe us anything. He sent His Son to die for us because He loves us - not because He owes us or even because that is what He ought to do. Romans 11:35 (NIV) rhetorically asks us, "Who has ever given to God, that God should repay them?" God created all things. Everything belongs to Him. He does not borrow; He lends. He gives.

As the psalmist says in Psalm 24:1 (NASB95), "The earth is the LORD's, and all it contains, the world, and those who dwell in it." Every single person on the planet belongs to God. He is dealing with all of His creation as the faithful Creator. 1 Corinthians 8:6 (NLT) reiterates His role as Creator, saying, "But for us, there is one God, the Father, by Whom all things were created, and for Whom we live. And there is one Lord, Jesus Christ, through Whom all things were created, and through Whom we live." God has done all things through His Son. Jesus is the image of the invisible God (Colossians 1:15). Let us come before Him today in awe and reverence. Let us bring glory that is due His great name!

The final verse of Romans 11 closes with this: "For from Him and through Him and to Him are all things. To Him be the glory forever. Amen." (Romans 11:36 NASB95) Everything God does is for His glory. He is worthy of all praise. All of His affections are set on you and me. He loves us! He will never leave us nor forsake us. He will never forsake His covenant nor the promises He has made to all who believe. Psalm 94:14 (NASB95) is God's promise to us, which says, "For the LORD will not abandon His people, nor will He forsake His inheritance." The Lord has not forgotten about Israel, and He has not forgotten about you. He will not abandon you, no matter what you are going through or what you have done in the past.

The Lord will not abandon the Jewish state of Israel either. No matter how many rockets pour into the land from the Gaza Strip - or from the north, south, or east - God's divine hand of protection is upon Israel. He will never leave her nor forsake her. The Bible tells us in Psalm 87:1-3 (NLT), "On the holy mountain stands the city founded by the LORD. He loves the city of Jerusalem more than any other city in Israel. O city of God, what glorious things are said of you!" From God's perspective, Jerusalem is the center of the world. God loves Jerusalem above all other cities on the earth. His eyes are glued to the city of David forever.

You and I are a part of God's inheritance. There is a piece of you that is attached to Israel because you are attached to the Lord. No matter where your birthplace is, what your nationality is, or what family you come from, if you are a follower of Jesus Christ, then you have a stake in the nation of Israel. What happens in Israel is personal because you are a Christian. When Israel suffers, the body of Christ suffers. When Israel thrives, the body of Christ thrives. The two are inseparable. Your Savior is from Israel. Your King was born in the Holy Land. Your heritage is from Zion. Your identity stems from the Middle East.

No wonder there is so much warfare in the Middle East. No wonder the battle between good and evil, right and wrong, rages on. The enemy knows His time is short (Revelation 12:12). The Risen King is coming back to Israel again soon! (Zechariah 14:4) Let us praise God for what He is doing in the Holy Land today. Let us invite the return of our Great King into Jerusalem. Let us praise Him and invite His Holy Presence to invade the land of Israel. Let us welcome the return of the Messiah through the Eastern Gate.

Come now Church and let us sing, "Open up, ancient gates! Open up, ancient doors, and let the King of glory enter. Who is the King of glory? The LORD, strong and mighty; the LORD, invincible in battle. Open up, ancient gates! Open up, ancient doors, and let the King of glory enter. Who is the King of glory? The LORD of Heaven's Armies— He is the King of glory." (Psalm 24:7-10 NLT)

REASON THREE

Because Seeing is Believing

The first time I traveled to Israel it changed the way I viewed the Bible and my Christian faith forever. My first reaction, along with most of my peers on my first trip, was to kiss the ground right after stepping off the airplane in Tel Aviv, Israel. The feelings and flood of emotions that come when you first step foot in the Holy Land for the first time ever is something that cannot be expressed using words. As a believer, I would equate it to how Neil Armstrong must have felt the first time he stepped foot on the moon. It is out of this world! There is nothing like visiting Israel for the first time.

I always encourage people to visit the Holy Land if they ever have the opportunity to. While I know not everyone can visit and that it is not cheap to travel overseas, when given the opportunity it can certainly be a life-changing trip. My third reason for standing with Israel is "because seeing is believing". Physically seeing the land of Israel only solidified the reason I wholeheartedly stand with Israel and the Jewish people who live there. To me, it was obvious Israel is "Jewish country". Growing up in west Texas country, I sometimes would hear people say, "This is God's country." The open country, clear skies, and beautiful sunsets were enough to convince me they were right!

Likewise, when I first visited Israel, I knew immediately I was in Hebrew country. I knew in my heart of hearts that the land was made for the Jewish people. While I have plenty of Scriptures to back up this feeling in my spirit, I am still in awe of how resilient the Jewish people are - even after enduring the Holocaust from hell less than a century ago. As the Israelis have warded off enemies on every side for decades, it is incredible how the nation continues to flourish. The cities are exuberantly filled with life and with people from around the world. Tourists from all over come to see the different sites and to learn more about the origins of their faith.

The story of how I actually found my way to Israel in the summer of 2009 is quite miraculous in and of itself. It all started a few months prior when a friend of mine was telling me about a man she met that was the director of Christians United for Israel (CUFI) on Campus at the time. She told me his name was Andrew Summey, and I had to meet him. His love for Israel was the same as mine. I had always talked about my love for Israel with friends at school and at church, but I had never visited. During this time I was in graduate school studying business, but during the summer I wanted to do something special before my final semester of college. I prayed about it and felt a tug in my heart to stay a few months in Manhattan (for those of you who have read my second book Breathe, the cover was inspired from a dream I had not long before this trip). I found a room for rent on the Upper West side, so I made plans for a part time job, reached out to others who already lived in New York that were in my circle of college friends, and scheduled the flight.

When I first arrived to the Big Apple, I was overwhelmed with excitement and marveled at the greatest city in the world. The huge skyscrapers, the boats and ferries, the subway trains, the airplanes and helicopters, and the hustle and bustle of people was breathtaking. I felt like I was in a movie! What's more, my apartment was just a few blocks from the Seinfeld restaurant I had seen on TV growing up. Of course it was one of the first diners I frequented during my temporary stay. The first few weeks I spent meeting new people and discovering different parts of the city. I found a great Bible study to attend each week, and the leader's name was Anthony DiMaio. Anthony had at one time worked on the New York Stock Exchange. Wall Street had always fascinated me as a B-school student; also, a guy who ministers in the prophetic had recently prophesied at church that one day I would go to Wall Street and reach powerful people for God's kingdom.

One night I was headed back to the apartment, and after I hopped off the subway I called a college friend back home. As I began to tell them about different experiences in the city, I asked them to pray for me. I remember that night as being one where I could feel my future destiny closer than ever before. As they began to pray, I saw in a vision (that is, on the movie screen of my mind) stars coming down over the nation's capitol building. It was so real and vivid that I told my friend after they finished praying. I went to bed that night wondering what the vision meant. The next morning I woke up to check my messages, and I had an email from Andrew Summey, the director of CUFI on Campus. He wrote me to ask if I would be interested in joining him and Christians from all over the country to attend the 4th Annual CUFI Summit at the capitol in Washington DC.

The message proceeded to inform me that Christians United for Israel (CUFI) was sponsoring select college students from all across the nation to attend the event. Travel and lodging were to be provided. First I rubbed my eyes to make sure I was reading correctly, then I wrote back accepting this gracious offer. After calling my friend and sharing the marvelous news - how it all coincided with the vision from the night before - I booked the 3 hour train ride from Grand Central Station to Washington DC. Not many days later I found myself shaking endless hands and meeting students, pastors, teachers, and political leaders from all over the world right outside the nation's capitol.

The event was filled with different guest speakers, including Israeli Prime Minister Benjamin Netanyahu via a video stream. I remember watching in awe as Netanyahu came on the big screen. He was very kind and expressed his gratitude from Israel for all we were doing to strengthen the US-Israel political alliance and to keep up the good work! Then there were different senators who would get up to speak. I remember one speaker concluding his speech, quoting Proverbs 9:10, which says, "The fear of the LORD is the beginning of wisdom, and knowledge of the Holy One is understanding." The verse packed a punch, as God has shown us through His Word that anyone who stands with Israel will be blessed, but woe to those who turn against her!

The CUFI Summit also included a nightly worship service, filled with prayers for the nation of Israel and for the salvation of the United States. Prayers for revival filled the conference room, as believers from all over the country sang and lifted up their cries to God for our nation's leaders. Throughout the day there were scheduled meetings with different Congress members from every state. I attended the meeting with Senator John Cornyn, who was one of the two Texas senators. Kay Bailey Hutchison, the other Texas senator, was not in, but Senator Cornyn spoke on her behalf. The meeting room was jam packed from wall to wall, as cameras flashed and recorders rolled. John Hagee, the founder of Christians United For Israel, introduced Senator Cornyn and thanked him for meeting with us. Hagee expressed his concern for the nation of Israel and the importance of the U.S. Congress' role in strengthening political ties with the only true democracy in the Middle East.

Then Senator Cornyn spoke and affirmed to everyone in the room that he and Senator Hutchison stood firmly with Israel. He mentioned several different political policies they supported that were pro-Israel legislation and thanked all of us for voicing our strong support for the Jewish state. After leaving the meeting I went back to the large conference room and heard other speakers, many of whom were active Congress members. During the lunch breaks, I would eat with different students and leaders involved with CUFI. It was so encouraging to meet other people who felt the same way I did about Israel.

One evening some of the CUFI students and I were hanging out on the west side of the capitol at the Capitol Reflecting Pool. As we stood there I started to pray under my breath. Then I heard the Holy Spirit tell me to start walking around the capitol. As I started walking I began lifting up different senators and representatives to the Lord. I prayed for our country. I prayed that God would bond Israel and the United States with an unbreakable tie - that God would raise up an entire generation of people who stood with Israel. The prayers continued to flow as I could feel God's presence each time I made a full lap around the Capitol Reflecting Pool. I walked symbolically seven times around the pool.

I had some time to sit by the reflecting pool and reflect on all the incredible experiences I was having. I felt deep in my spirit that one day in the future I would be back to DC. Since that noteworthy evening I have met other legislators over the past several years. I have not seen some of the dreams and things the Lord has shown me come to pass yet. However, I know at just the right time God is going to take me back to the halls of Congress, only next time it will not be as a student. Psalm 33:12 tells us, "Blessed is the nation whose God is the LORD." As the battle rages on Capitol Hill, the spiritual war of the enemy trying to strip America of her Judeo-Christian principles that have made her great to begin with will only escalate.

As believers, we need to be praying for our nation's leaders. We need to pray our legislators and judges will honor God's Word and support policies that are good, just, and Biblically sound. While the United States is not a theocracy, many of the fundamental values that are woven into the fabric of our laws are based on Biblical truths. While I visited Washington DC, I knew I was standing before the most powerful earthly government in the world. What happens in DC impacts the entire earth. I was encouraged walking around the different sites and seeing quotes that clearly point to faith in God.

The Washington Monument has Scriptures like "Holiness to the Lord" (Isaiah 23:18), "Search the Scriptures" (John 5:39), and "The memory of the just is blessed" (Proverbs 10:7) inscribed on it. On the capstone is written the Latin phrase "Laus Deo", which means "Praise be to God". It is no wonder the United States has grown into the most powerful and wealthy nation in human history. Our American forefathers were rich in faith and truly trusted in the Lord to bless our country. While America is certainly not perfect, I believe God has honored our declaration "In God We Trust" that is inscribed on all of our currency and in our House and Senate Chambers.

After sightseeing and attending scheduled events at the CUFI Summit, I returned to New York. I spent the next few weeks working with an acting coach and looking into print modeling. One of the purposes of my visit to New York was to explore the world of acting, modeling, and the media industry in general. One day I was having a bite to eat, and a Jewish man named Ronald approached me. He told me I looked like a model, and I had that "southern gentleman" look. He then went on to tell me he had a collection of jewelry that he wanted me to model for him. I was a little skeptical at first, but as we continued to talk I learned that his father owned a shop in the diamond district, his grandparents had fled from the holocaust, and his mother had tragically taken her own life when he was younger.

One of the things that really amazed me about Ronald was his passion and zeal for life. He was a true artist, and he had a genuine love for God. Ronald Grunberg was also one of my first encounters with the many Jewish people living in New York City. I was so fascinated by Ronald's brilliance and to be honest, his Jewishness. He just stood out from the ordinary. It was through this divine appointment that God really spoke to my heart concerning the Jewish people. We hung out a few times, and he shared with me more of his handcrafted jewelry collection. We also went to the roof of his apartment complex where he took pictures of me showcasing the men's cufflinks and other jewelry.

On our last day to hang out shortly before I returned to Texas at the end of the summer break, something only God could have supernaturally orchestrated happened. Ronald was showing me his century old Hebrew Bible his mom gave him. He is Jewish so it did not include the New Testament. He showed me with a heavy heart the place where his mother took her life. Clearly, Ronald and his mother were very close. Then a man came around the corner as Ronald was showing me the Hebrew Bible. This man was one of Ronald's neighbors and a very bold Christian man. He began to tell Ronald that Jesus Christ died for him, and he needed to put His faith in Jesus. He told how Jesus Christ fulfilled the Law and the Prophets of the Old Testament, the very Hebrew book he was holding!

As I stood there in awe and wonder, I was thanking the Lord under my breath for sending this man to witness to Ronald. Ronald knew I was a Christian, but I never gave Ronald a straight-forward, blunt altar call like this outspoken Christian neighbor! Ronald listened to the good neighbor, and I don't know if Ronald ever made a decision for Christ that day or not. What I do know is that God had His eyes set on this Jewish man who had been well-acquainted with sorrow. I share the story about Ronald, because it is through this divine encounter that God gave me a soft heart for the Jewish people. The older generation of Jewish people really knew the Holocaust firsthand. For many of them, the generation before them (and their grandparents' generation) were lost during World War II. Others had fled to the States for safety, and now they and their children, like Ronald, live in New York City.

I prayed often for the Jewish people when living in New York, sometimes for hours. My whole life I have felt a divine calling to minister to, to serve, and to love the Jewish people as a Christian. There are approximately 15 million Jewish people in the world today. Of those 15 million, around 7 million live in the USA and 7 million live in Israel. Jews in New York City account for 13% of the city's population, making it the largest Jewish community in the world outside of Israel. The other major city in the United States that has a large population of Jewish people is in Los Angeles, California. Los Angeles has the second largest Jewish population in the United States, and the fifth largest population of any city in the world. It is no wonder I have always felt called to New York City and Los Angeles!

A few weeks before the end of my stay in New York, I received another surprise message from Andrew Summey, the director of CUFI on Campus. He informed me that a college student had dropped out of the first-ever "Walk to Remember" overseas trip to Poland and Israel. The trip included staying a full week in Poland and a full week in Israel, touring different sites from the Holocaust in Poland and then Israel, all expenses paid - travel, meals, and lodging. He told me 40 select students had been signed up, but he had an opened space available last minute. He asked if I knew anyone who was already living in New York who had a passport, as the trip was in just 8 days. I wrote him back and told him I was a student, I had my passport in my hand, and yes I was very interested! My heart started to pound as I waited for his response.

Going to Israel was a huge dream I had always had growing up. Waiting for Andrew to respond felt like the longest few minutes of my life. He then responded, "That would be great!" As I leaped for joy in my apartment, praising God, a flood of tears began to flow, as I could not believe God could be this good to me. An all-expenses paid trip to Poland and Israel to learn more about the history of Israel and the Jewish people?! A dream come true! Looking back I can see how the hand of God was moving me into the perfect place at the perfect time. CUFI on Campus did not even exist until 2009, the very same year I just happened to be staying in NYC. CUFI had never sent students overseas before in its history as a pro-Israel grassroots organization.

What's even more profound is how highly selective this special trip was. Hundreds of students from all over the country had submitted to go on this trip of 40 college students who possessed strong leadership qualities. For me to have a free pass onto the trip last minute was nothing short of God's miraculous hand at work. Once I filled out all the paperwork and began to prepare for the trip, I really had no idea what to expect. All I knew to do was pack my bags for hot weather and be prepared to take the subway to JFK Airport in a week. Leading up to the trip the Lord had continued to show me great things concerning the future. I had no idea going to Israel was the next big surprise He had for me!

The prophet Jeremiah tells us in Jeremiah 33:2-3 (NASB95), "Thus says the LORD who made the earth, the LORD who formed it to establish it, the LORD is His name, 'Call to Me and I will answer you, and I will tell you great and mighty things, which you do not know.'" I did not know that summer I was going to visit Washington DC, all expenses paid. I did not know I was going to be handed a two week tour of a lifetime (also all expenses paid) when I first took a leap of faith and decided to stay in New York City for a summer. All I knew is I could feel the Holy Spirit challenging me to dream bigger and to believe that anything is possible. In order for us to see the miraculous, sometimes we must be in a position to need a miracle. When I stayed in New York that summer, I was humbled. Being from the rural country, I could not wrap my head around the big city. There was so much to see and learn about.

All I knew was God is even greater than Manhattan. He has the entire world and everything in it sitting in the palm of His hand. Nothing is too difficult for the Lord! When I loaded my suitcase and bags onto the subway to take the train ride to the airport, I was so nervous. I had never been to the Holy Land, more or less with complete strangers. When I finally arrived at JFK, CUFI had set up a conference room at the hotel airport for the meet and greet before flying out the next day. In the conference room there were table name plates set out with the name of each student and the university they represented. After meeting and greeting with different people around the room Andrew Summey got up to speak.

He shared with us some details about the trip. He told us we were going to be touring a lot of sites and going to be covering a lot of ground in a short amount of time. (Two weeks later I can attest to this; my head was reeling with all the new information I had crammed in from the trip!) He introduced us to our main tour guide Avi. Avi was Jewish and very well-versed for nearly any question we had throughout the trip. We were also introduced to David Brog, a cool-spirited attorney, who was also the executive director of CUFI at the time. David had studied at both

Princeton and Harvard. He had authored a book we all had entitled, "Standing With Israel: Why Christians Support the Jewish State" (2006). David was one of my favorite people to be around during the trip because he was easy going by nature and really cared about us as students being trained to be well-informed activists for Israel.

Another key leader we were introduced to the first night before flying out was Holocaust survivor Irving Roth. Irving Roth was a living testament to the mercy of God. Irving had survived Auschwitz as a young boy, and he would be sharing many of his experiences along the way. That night all the students became better acquainted with one another. I met several students from around the country who loved the Lord, and we would often pray together at different times throughout the trip. All of the students came from different Christian religious affiliated backgrounds, so we didn't always all see eye to eye on different doctrines and teachings.

When we boarded the plane to cross the pond, it reminded me of my first overseas trip I had taken just a year before. In 2008, when I finished undergraduate studies, I flew to Mozambique, Africa to serve at an orphanage in Zimpeto just outside of the capital city Maputo for two weeks. I remembered how long the flight felt and then having to sit for several hours in the London airport during a layover; I had been overly amused that "fish and chips" in London was not fried catfish and potato chips (chips are french fries, in case you might be wondering). As we buckled up for takeoff, all of the students were excited. Some of us were reading the required reading material given to us when we signed up to go on the trip. Some were listening to music on their headphones. Others, like myself, were conversing with their peers next to them.

During the flight, I had several interesting conversations with my new friends. One notable conversation I had was with the executive director, David Brog. While talking to David, he asked me more about my life and told me more about himself. As we were talking, I began to tell him how I was raised to love Israel and the Jewish people; I said I was so passionate for the Jewish people that I would literally take a bullet for them. His eyes got really big when I said I was ready and willing to sacrifice my own life for the sake of a Jewish person, and he asked how I came to love Israel and the Jewish people so much. I told him I was taught from a very young age that we, as Christians, were called to pray for and love the Jewish people.

I then told David the story about how I almost attended Princeton University, where he had studied, but how God turned my heart to stay in Texas and study at Hardin-Simmons University. I told him my college experience had been extraordinary at HSU, but I still had some regrets about not attending an Ivy League school. He consoled me by telling me I was probably much better off for having studied at a Christian university in the South with such strong Biblical values than at a liberal university. I could tell David had an appreciation for the southern values that I may have taken for granted growing up.

When we finally landed on the ground in Warsaw, Poland, the intensive on-site tours began. We first visited a World War II museum and watched a black and white film about how the first Jewish ghettos began to form in Europe when the Nazi's overtook Poland. We then visited the most run down parts of Warsaw where Jews were forced to live. Warsaw had by far the largest ghetto, where half a million Jews were segregated - shut in by walls, fences, and barbed wire. No one was permitted to enter or leave without special permission. The ghettos were the gathering place in Poland for the Jewish people before they were eventually deported to the concentration camps.

Disease was rampant in these overcrowded districts and many even died of starvation. As I stood and listened to the tour guides and saw pictures and video footage, often in horror, I could not help but think, "Where in the world were the Americans? Where were my grandparents? How did WE let this happen?" The American, the proud defender of freedom for all, within me was furious! I could not understand how the world just stood by and let the evil continue. During the trip, I heard a famous quote our guides would say that resonated with all that we were seeing, which is: "The only thing necessary for the triumph of evil is for good men to do nothing." While we heard heroic stories both from Irving Roth, the Holocaust survivor, and our tour guide Avi, it still was nauseating to think the Holocaust could have been prevented had more people around the world stepped up to defend the Jewish people and other Holocaust victims.

While in Poland, I remember the eerie feeling of a post-World War II heaviness over the land. It was similar to the feeling you have when you visit a massive graveyard. The cruel acts that had occurred less than 70 years ago in the land could still be felt and seen by what remained. While in Poland, we also visited other historic landmarks so as to not just see the doom and gloom of the Holocaust only. One of my favorite places we toured was the Royal Castle in Warsaw. The building itself is massive. We walked through room after room - each palatial room covered in different artwork and unique interior design. It reminded me of the Scripture where Jesus tells His disciples in John 14:2 (ESV), "In My Father's house are many rooms. If it were not so, would I have told you that I go to prepare a place for you?"

While sitting in the courtyard of the Royal Castle, many of the students and myself were very quiet. What we had seen and heard at the museum and the ghettos was disturbing. Every day we would take time to reflect. Our leaders would often prepare us for some of the things we were going to see and learn about, as the events that took place were mentally and emotionally overwhelming, and some of us would need more time than others to process and reflect what we just experienced. They would also encourage us to not forget what we had learned but to use the experience constructively to make the world a better place once we returned home. After spending the first few days in Warsaw, we then traveled south to Krakow. It was on our way south that we were especially warned about what we were going to see.

As I prepared myself for visiting the Auschwitz concentration camp the next day outside of Krakow, I could hardly imagine what it was going to be like. I had no idea how I would react when I physically saw the camp I had only read and studied about in school. I remember when we first rolled up outside the camp, everyone became very quiet. It was as if we all knew together to have reverence for the lives that were lost and also for their remaining loved ones who might be visiting that day. When the tour of Auschwitz began, I felt ok emotionally. Up to this point of the trip I had yet to really cry. We walked from site to site. We saw the skeletal barracks where the prisoners stayed. We learned how the Nazi soldiers would trick incoming train carts of Jews by telling them they would first take a shower in the gas chambers. They were to remove their clothing and their valuables.

I remember at one point of the tour, to my horror, there were rooms full of children's shoes, clothes, toys, and even their hair piled to the very high ceilings. The Nazis made sure to capitalize on all material possessions at these extermination camps. Irving Roth, who had survived Auschwitz, shared different stories during the tour of the camp as well. He was a nine year old boy, and God gave him favor in the eyes of the Nazi soldiers. He fed and tended to the horses. Irving also told about the days leading up to the American soldiers arriving at the camp to liberate the prisoners. That very day he thought he was going to die, as bombs and missiles were going off. The war was intense and the Nazis were fleeing.

Irving said when he saw the first American soldiers, it was like seeing the coming Messiah! These freedom fighters were his salvation. My eyes teared as I could finally see hope in the midst of the nightmare. Adolf Hitler's sick goal was to actually level the concentration camps and pretend like they never existed and nothing had ever happened. However, the Allies got to the camps before he could eliminate the evidence. Sadly, today there are enemies of Israel who want to eliminate the Jews. There are people who claim the Holocaust never happened. While you and I may think the world will never believe such ludicrous statements, we might ought to think again. The same devil that led Hitler by the hand is leading the world.

The anti-Semitic spirit that dwelt in Hitler still dwells in political leaders and in other people of great power. The way we combat this evil spirit is by speaking up. The men, women, and children who were murdered at these concentration camps cannot speak for themselves today, but we surely can!

Proverbs 31:8-9 (ESV) says, "Open your mouth for the mute, for the rights of all who are destitute. Open your mouth, judge righteously, defend the rights of the poor and needy." It is up to us, Church, to declare the truth about what happened at places like Auschwitz. It is up to us to defend the rights of all who have no voice.

When we stood in front of the furnace ovens and learned how the prisoners had to burn bodies all day, Irving Roth told us the smell of burning flesh was the worst smell on earth. Of course this smell wreaked throughout the camp. The death toll began to escalate even more at the concentration camps as the tide of the battle in World War II began to shift. The climax of my emotions during the whole trip came when I stood in front of a monument at Auschwitz in a field that read, "To the memory of the men, women, and children who fell victim to the Nazi genocide. Here lie their ashes. May their souls Rest In Peace." The spot I stood was where over 1 million Jews' ashes were buried and scattered.

It was here in this place that I finally began to sob. The tears flowed as I allowed my soul to mourn the murder of millions of innocent victims. I know if I was grieved over what took place during World War II, that surely the Lord was even more so. The Bible tells us that Jesus, our Messiah, was all too familiar with grief and sorrow. Isaiah 53:3 (NLT) says, "He was despised and rejected— a man of sorrows, acquainted with deepest grief. We turned our backs on him and looked the other way. He was despised, and we did not care." I am sure those who were destined to die at Auschwitz must have felt the same way. I can imagine the children were terrified, as they had to leave everything behind, crammed in rail carts having no idea where they were really going.

I believe God, in His great mercy and righteous judgment, turned the history of hell created by the most evil Nazi regime around when He stirred the hearts of His people to re-establish the Jewish state of Israel in 1948. While what happened leading up to and during WW2 can never be undone, it can be prevented from happening again if God's people will stand up for what is right and do something about it. It is when good people do nothing, when good people merely attend to their own lives and neglect standing up for those who are being mistreated in the world, that horrible things like the Holocaust and genocide happen. God has not called us to live ingrown. He has called us to be a lighthouse to the world.

After our final tour in Poland, we caught the red-eye flight to Tel Aviv, Israel. The leaders told us to try and sleep as best we could on the plane because touring started right after we landed. The next morning when the plane landed we all hopped onto the tarmac in excitement. We were finally here! Some of us were audacious enough to even kiss the ground as an outward expression of our deep love for Israel. Even our lack of sleep could not contain the excitement of finally seeing the land where our Lord and Savior once walked and taught. When we loaded up on the tour bus, we went straight to touring. No naps. No unpacking at the youth hostel. We were on a tight schedule.

The tour of Israel was day and night from touring Poland. Poland, a place filled with horrific sites of the past and tragic memoirs of those who survived (or didn't), was opposite from Israel. Israel was a land full of hope and joy. Our tour guide said to always remember, Israel became a nation despite the Holocaust. Even the Holocaust could not terminate the resilient spirit of the Jewish people, and anyone who has witnessed the vibrancy of Israel and her people in the present day would agree. Despite all of the horror less than a century ago, Israel stands stronger today than ever before.

One of the first things we learned about was the different wars Israel won against Arab forces in order to solidify her rightful place in the Middle East. In 1948-1949, Israel and Arab forces clashed after the UN voted to partition the British mandate of Palestine into two separate states: a Jewish state and an Arab state. On May 14, 1948, the day before British forces withdrew, Israel declared independence. The United States President Harry S. Truman recognized Israel as a nation on the same day. The very next day Arab forces from Egypt, Transjordan (Jordan), Iraq, Syria, and Lebanon occupied areas in eastern and southern Palestine and captured eastern Jerusalem. Israelis successfully withstood repeat Arab attacks. By 1949, Israel had reclaimed all of the Negev (southern Israel), except the Gaza Strip.

As the tour guide explained how Israel continually warded off her enemies and grew stronger, anyone who knew the Lord and the Scriptures knew it was the hand of God giving the Israeli fighters success. We know whose land belongs to who, because we have a Bible full of detailed descriptions telling the world so. No matter how many Arab nations try to attack Israel, they are not going to win because really they are not warring with Israel or the IDF (Israel Defense Force); they are warring with God and His Word. As long as God's hand is on the land that belongs to Israel, no one - not even the USA with its powerful army (all due respect to our incredible armed forces) - can defeat what God has ordained.

There was another war with Egypt when Egyptian President Gamal Abdel Nasser nationalized the Suez Canal in 1956. He barred Israel from using this vital waterway between Europe and Asia, as well as blockaded Israel's southern port at Elat. France and Britain owned much of the Suez Canal waterway so they struck a deal with Israel to attack Egypt. Israel invaded the Sinai Peninsula of Egypt in October 1956 and within 5 days captured vital cities in the peninsula just east of the Suez Canal. By March 1957 Israeli troops withdrew after intervention from Britain and France, whereby a UN Emergency Force was stationed in the area. Egyptian forces were defeated on all fronts.

As I listened to the different war stories from tour guides and saw pictures of valiant Israeli soldiers fighting for freedom in the midst of what I would consider very oppressive Arab religious regimes, I just imagined all of the stories I heard growing up about great people of faith fighting for the land like when Joshua entered the Promised Land, Samson conquered the Philistines, and David took out Goliath. The history of Israel truly is His story. God's divine hand has always ruled over the land of Israel. It is His Spirit that has given Israel and the Israel Defense Force (IDF) success. While we were touring we met several IDF soldiers. One of the soldier's names was Ohad. Ohad really enjoyed hanging out with us, so he joined us when he could during our time in Israel.

I remember visiting different sites where missiles had been launched from Gaza; one particular area was near an Israeli school yard. These homemade missiles had been gathered into a pile, and we stood in front of the pile of missiles listening to our guide tell us how students and families had to flee to different shelters when Palestinians would stage arsenal attacks just across the border in Gaza. There were sirens set up so children and teachers would know when to flee to the shelters. Israeli citizens had to be vigilant, as these strikes could happen in a moment's notice. The difference between today and the years building up to World War II (and the Holocaust) is now Israel has its own army.

God has turned the tide of the battle against the Jews' enemies by restoring the Jewish state of Israel. To this day there are people groups who still wish all Jewish people dead. It's both disgusting and sad. The hatred engrained in Israel's surrounding neighbors towards them is palpable. Benjamin Netanyahu said it best concerning the issue right now in the Middle East. He says, "If the Arabs put down their weapons today, there would be no more violence. If the Jews put down their weapons today, there would be no more Israel." The difference between Israel and the Arabs is that Israel seeks peace. The Arabs seek annihilation of the Jewish people. We have seen this kind of hatred before in the eyes of Adolf Hitler. This time it comes in the form of true radical Islam.

Many years ago it was prophesied that the descendants of Ishmael would always live in hostility with Israel. Genesis 16:11-12 (NIV) says, "The angel of the LORD also said to her [Hagar]: 'You are now pregnant and you will give birth to a son. You shall name him Ishmael, for the LORD has heard of your misery. He will be a wild donkey of a man; his hand will be against everyone and everyone's hand against him, and he will live in hostility toward all his brothers.'" To this day the Arab nations live in hostility towards both one another and towards Israel.

The only way any true freedom could ever come to the Middle East is through spiritual revival - that is, the preaching and accepting of the gospel that Jesus Christ came to save us from our sins. There are pockets of revival happening in the Middle East, and we celebrate that! However, there will be no lasting peace without Jesus Christ. The same is true in our own lives. Jesus is the Prince of all peace. If we want more peace in our lives, then we must make Him Lord of every area of our lives. When we do our best to adhere to the teachings of Christ and offer ourselves to Him on a daily basis, only then are we going to walk more fully in the freedom and in the power of the Holy Spirit.

There were several times during the trip I had spiritual encounters with the Lord and His angels. The fact that we were in the Holy Land made these spiritual experiences all the more awesome! One night while getting ready in my room to have dinner for Shabbat (Jews begin celebrating the Sabbath on Friday night at sunset), I bowed down on the floor to pray. I was so excited to be in Israel, and I wanted to make the most of my time there - so I prayed. I prayed over the trip, over the students and leaders, and over all the places we were going to see. Before I finished praying, I began to pray that the Lord would send His most powerful angels to be with me. All of the sudden, while I was praying, I began to ask the Lord to send Gabriel to be near to me while on the trip (see Daniel 9:21 and Luke 1:19). Sure, it was a bold prayer. Then again, I was in the Holy Land so why not pray bold!

After I got up off the floor, I proceeded downstairs for dinner. As I left the room I saw one of the girls on the trip, who was a Spirit-filled woman passionate about the Lord. She stopped me in the hallway and looked at me intently. Then she said, "McKade, your face is glowing. I just see the angel Gabriel in your face right now!" She kept saying I looked like the angel Gabriel. She wouldn't stop saying it. I was blown away. The Lord had answered my prayer almost instantly. I don't know why I asked for the Lord to send Gabriel, one of His most powerful angels, except that the Holy Spirit was prompting me to do so. I did not pray to Gabriel, as we know we pray directly to God Himself, but I did seek divine protection from the Lord through His angel and servant Gabriel.

Throughout the trip I had other visions and divine encounters like the one I had that night before Shabbat dinner. One of the students on the trip would play worship music on the guitar at night. Many of us would join him to sing and praise the Lord for all He has done. During these student-led worship services God would show me different visions while we stared into the dark night across the land of Israel. I would often see a gate with angels surrounding it in my visions. In my spirit I could hear the Lord saying He was coming through the Eastern Gate (see Ezekiel 44:1-2, Zechariah 14:4, and Acts 1:9-11).

While in Jerusalem I stood at a distance observing the Eastern Gate that has been sealed up. There are graves in front of the Eastern Gate. These graves are a massive Muslim cemetery, seemingly set up as an attempt to defile and defy the Messiah's return. However, I am confident the Muslim's gravesite will not stop our Lord and Savior Jesus Christ from marching straight through the Golden Gate to His rightful throne! When the enemy tries to mock the Lord, the Lord always gets the last laugh. Psalm 37:12-13 (NLT) tells us, "The wicked plot against the godly; they snarl at them in defiance. But the Lord just laughs, for He sees their day of judgment coming."

The physical warfare that is so prevalent in the Middle East is a mirror of what is happening in the unseen spiritual realm. If our spiritual eyes were completely opened, we would be amazed at the spiritual forces warring over Israel. It might look something like the creatures we read about in the book of Revelation! The physical pile of missiles I saw launched at Israel are a reflection of the activity of what Satan wants to do to the land of Israel. The good news is God has the final say. What God has started in Israel, He is going to finish. While we learned about the wars of Israel and the surrounding threats of her neighbors, we also got to have some fun. One of my favorite things to do was to go tubing down the Jordan River.

It was at the Jordan River that the real fun on the trip began. Floating down the Jordan River reminded me of John the Baptist and the spiritual significance of water baptism. There was a sense of awe floating on the same river Jesus was baptized in. It was the same river that supernaturally parted for the prophets Elijah and Elisha to cross over (2 Kings 2:8) and for the priests and all of Israel as they crossed into the Promised Land (Joshua 3). I can't imagine what it was like to witness a river full of water to just stop flowing and the ground beneath to dry up in order for God's people to cross over safely. Israel truly is the land of signs, wonders, and miracles!

Another profound place we visited was Ein Gedi. Ein Gedi was one of my favorite places to visit during the entire trip. One of the tour guides told us that Ein Gedi is where David hid from King Saul (1 Samuel 24:1-2). Ein Gedi was absolutely beautiful - an oasis and nature reserve just west of the Dead Sea. Ein Gedi served as a water source during Biblical times. While at Ein Gedi we hiked a short distance to reach David's waterfall and pools where people were swimming. It was hot that day so some of us went ahead and took a dip.

While in the area we also went down to the Dead Sea to take mud baths and "float". The reason I don't say swim is because it's virtually impossible to swim in the Dead Sea. The Dead Sea is the lowest place on earth at 430.5 meters below sea level. The extremely high density causes the human body to seemingly float when in the water. The water is so salty (9.6 times saltier than the ocean) that you cannot open your eyes underwater. I accidentally did once, and it burned! Many people take mud baths in the Dead Sea, as it is therapeutic for the skin. What's more fascinating is that even though the Dead Sea was hot and sunny, the skin did not burn very easily because harmful UV rays are mostly filtered before reaching the extremely low elevation levels.

While floating in the Dead Sea with mud caked all over our bodies, we looked at the geography around us. Across the sea there was an interesting looking landmark. It looked like the statue of a woman. The pillar of salt we were seeing is called "Lot's Wife" and is located on Mount Sodom. I believe this landmark is more than a coincidence. It may or may not have literally been Lot's wife when she turned back and became a pillar of salt (see Genesis 19:26), but it certainly is a God-wink! The more I sat in the water and floated (without any floaties!), the more I realized I was more than likely floating right on top of what used to be the ancient cities of Sodom and Gomorrah before they were destroyed.

Another touring spot that really brought the Scriptures to life was visiting the city of Jerusalem. One of my favorite things we did there was walk through the narrow, dark water channel built by Hezekiah during the impending siege. Hezekiah's tunnel was built by King Hezekiah in order to prepare for the siege by the Assyrian army who was led by Sennacherib. The walk through Hezekiah's tunnel took about 20 minutes (583 yards long). As we all rolled up our shorts and trekked through the knee-high water, the tour guide told us the history of how King Hezekiah built the incredible tunnel system running under the City of David in order to keep water flowing to the city during the siege.

During the break between scheduled touring, we would shop and check out some of the local restaurants. One of the most popular dishes served is hummus and pita bread. While in Israel I had to indulge in all Israel had to offer. We ate hummus and at Shabbat meals on the weekend we would all bang the table and sing, "Shabbat shalom! Shabbat shalom! Shabbat, Shabbat, Shabbat shalom!" To this day I sometimes find myself humming and singing this simple Sabbath day celebration song. Another thing I noticed was nearly all of the food was kosher. One day we were near a McDonald's so I decided to go in and order a cheeseburger. Much to my surprise, the hamburger patties tasted like real beef! It was the best McDonald's hamburger I had ever had. I attributed it to the strict kosher laws - although I have no proof this Israeli McDonald's was using better beef than a McDonald's back home.

While in the City of David, we all had the opportunity to pray at the Western Wall. After I put on my kippah in honor of the Jewish tradition, I walked up to the Western Wall and began to pray next to my peers. The tour guide encouraged us to write a prayer on a piece of paper and stick it in the wall, as is tradition for all who pilgrimage to Jerusalem. My note contained several things on it, including the petition for God to build an inseparable bond between my country and Israel. I also prayed for the peace of Jerusalem, that I might always keep Zion in my thoughts and prayers. Psalm 137:5-6 (ESV) declares, "If I forget you, O Jerusalem, let my right hand forget its skill! Let my tongue stick to the roof of my mouth, if I do not remember you, if I do not set Jerusalem above my highest joy!"

Another spot we visited in Jerusalem was the place believed to be the empty tomb of Jesus. The Garden Tomb was one of the most refreshing and beautiful sites to see. You could feel the Holy Spirit right as you stepped onto the grounds. I remember during various times of the day speakers around the city would blare an Islamic call to worship. The sound was disturbing and certainly felt demonic to me, so when we visited the Garden Tomb it was refreshing to be in a place where the presence of God could be felt so strongly.

While I could go on and on about all the different sites and experiences we had throughout the trip, the most important thing to note is Israel is real. The sites and the testaments they hold to about the events that took place in Israel are real, and therefore our Bibles are real! The stories and testimonies contained from Genesis to Revelation are all true stories. They are not fiction or fairy tales. At one point of the trip, we stood next to the Sea of Galilee and listened as our tour guide read from the gospels a teaching of Jesus. The bank where we stood was likely near where Jesus had taught. Looking over the sea one could imagine Jesus sending His disciples across before walking on water later that evening during a tumultuous storm.

Driving through the open hills and valleys was an awesome site to see. One day we were on the bus, and the driver got on the microphone to tell us we were driving through Jezreel Valley where the battle of Armageddon (which is the Hebrew expression for Mount Megiddo) was to take place in the End Times. Revelation 16:16 (KJV) says, "And he gathered them together into a place called in the Hebrew tongue Armageddon." Of course I immediately sat up and looked around at the fertile plains surrounding us and began to imagine the armies piled high who were to be defeated by the Lord. No matter what part of Israel we visited, there was always a story to tell. The land is filled with thousands of years of history testifying to the reality that God is real, and that there is only one true God: the God of Israel.

The more you see, the more you cannot help but to believe. We went on several hikes during the trip - the most notable being the hike up Masada. Masada sits 450 meters high and takes over an hour to climb. When we reached the top of Masada, everyone was out of breath. However, the views from so high above were extraordinary. Atop the mesa-like plateau sits an ancient fortress, famous for the last stand of the Zealots in the Jewish revolt against Rome (around 66-73 AD). After learning more about this final stand according to the writings of Jewish historian Flavius Josephus and from our tour guide, we decided to give ourselves a break and take the cable cars down the steep plateau.

The grandeur of the Roman empire could be seen especially when we visited Caesarea in north central Israel. This historic port city of King Herod still has incredible remains displaying the wonders of Roman port engineering. The Romans had built an artificial harbor with massive concrete blocks, and an aqueduct brought water from springs almost

10 miles away. The amphitheater was also fun to visit. Students would speak on the stage, and their voice could be heard clearly at a distance (no microphone or sound equipment needed!). We also saw along the beautiful beach the hippodrome where Roman horse races took place.

After two full weeks of site seeing - all the while laughing, crying, contemplating, and having good clean fun - the entire CUFI team was exhausted. There was lots of snoring on the long flight home! When I stepped foot in New York City again, my brain was a pile of mush. For months, I found myself processing all that I had witnessed in Poland and Israel - not to mention my awesome and overwhelming three month experience in the Big Apple.

If you have never been to Israel, I encourage you to go. If you are unable to travel, find ways to learn more about the different sites in the Holy Land. I assure you, it will bring the Scriptures to life in a whole new light - because seeing is believing!

REASON FOUR

Israel is the Apple of God's Eye

All the way back in the book of Deuteronomy, the Lord speaks through His servant Moses concerning the Hebrew people. After Moses finished instructing the people of Israel all of the Torah, or Old Testament Law, the Lord commissions Joshua in Deuteronomy 31:23 (NASB95) saying, "Be strong and courageous, for you shall bring the sons of Israel into the land which I swore to them, and I will be with you." At this point in the Scriptures, the mantle of leadership is being passed from Moses to Joshua. It is interesting that one of the first things the Lord desires to impart to Joshua is a strong and courageous spirit.

It was so important for Joshua to know who he was as the leader of Israel and who Israel was in the eyes of God. The land Israel was entering was filled with powerful nations. As one of the original twelve spies, Joshua had seen the strong and fortified cities. He had seen the mighty men and giant warriors living in the land. However, Joshua also knew the promises of God. Having been born in the land of Goshen in Egypt, Joshua had seen the miraculous works of the Lord his entire life. He knew the 10 plagues. He saw the Red Sea part. He ate manna from heaven everyday and watched waters miraculously flow from a barren rock. He understood the awesome power of God in times of adversity.

One of the last things Moses teaches Joshua and the Israelites before passing away is a song the Lord gave him while in the Tent of Meeting. The Lord warned both Moses and Joshua in the Tabernacle that the Israelites would rebel against God's commandments once they entered the land of milk and honey and began to prosper. The Lord tells them Israel would provoke Him to anger by serving false gods and bring calamity upon themselves. In order to attest to why all of Israel's troubles and sorrows would come (that is, because of their rebellion towards the Lord), God gives Moses a song to recite for all of Israel to memorize.

The Song of Moses (Deuteronomy 32:1-43) is a dynamic song and poem given to Moses before his death on Mount Nebo. In the song, the Lord details how despite Israel's rebellious heart God's covenant with Jacob has never changed. The song served and still serves as a reminder of God's faithfulness to Israel. When a young Hebrew boy would sing the song, from his youth the child would sing about his heritage as a descendant of Israel. Deuteronomy 32:7-8 (NIV) says, "Remember the days of old; consider the generations long past. Ask your father and he will tell you, your elders, and they will explain to you. When the Most High gave the nations their inheritance, when He divided all mankind, He set up boundaries for the peoples according to the number of the sons of Israel."

From the beginning God had boundaries established for the nation of Israel. Furthermore, every nation on the earth has been divided just as the Lord has seen fit. There is no government or nation that is beyond the control of our God. Before Jesus came to usher in the new covenant of grace, God chose Israel - the descendants of Jacob - to be His chosen possession and to be His lighthouse to the world. Later on, after Christ, all people groups have been grafted into this chosen race of people. It is through Christ we are all made one family of God.

The Apostle Paul tells us in the New Testament, "So I bow in prayer before the Father from whom every family in heaven and on earth gets its true name." (Ephesians 3:14-15 NCV) God has named each and every person who is to ever live. You have a name that was ordained to be yours that is from the Lord. You are no accident, nor are you a surprise, to God! Your life has been carefully crafted and mapped out by the Creator. You are who God says you are, and your true identity can only be found in Him and in who He says you are in His Word. As a Christian, you are the apple of God's eye. You are the one God cherishes above all else. You are God's favorite child!

Knowing this should make you feel special as a believer and as a child of God. Knowing this should also make you want to help others realize their enormous value to the Lord. The Bible first makes mention of Israel being the apple of His eye in the Song of Moses. Deuteronomy 32:9-10 (ESV) says, "But the LORD's portion is His people, Jacob His allotted heritage. He found him in a desert land, and in the howling waste of the wilderness; He encircled him, He cared for him, He kept him as the apple of His eye." Wow! What powerful words from the Creator of the world! Visualize for a moment the great I AM walking through the desert land and coming upon Jacob while he slept on the ground, with a rock for his pillow (Genesis 28:11).

The LORD immediately had compassion for Jacob and chose him as a son. God chose Jacob to be the one He would make His name known through. Like a father imparting what he knows to his son and leaving his son the entire inheritance, God chose Jacob and his descendants to be His own inheritance. You and I share in this inheritance given to Jacob through Christ. Just as the Lord chose Israel out of all the nations, He chose you to be His own divine possession. He hand picked you to be His child! The promises God has made to Israel are for you also.

Romans 8:14-17 (NLT) says, "For all who are led by the Spirit of God are children of God. So you have not received a spirit that makes you fearful slaves. Instead, you received God's Spirit when He adopted you as His own children. Now we call Him, 'Abba, Father.' For His Spirit joins with our spirit to affirm that we are God's children. And since we are His children, we are His heirs. In fact, together with Christ we are heirs of God's glory. But if we are to share His glory, we must also share His suffering." The slavery mentality was a yoke that had to be broken off of the Israelites as they were in the desert. For 400 years the Hebrew people were oppressed and mistreated in Egypt (Acts 7:6).

As you can imagine, the people had terrible memories of Egyptians beating them and speaking to them harshly. Moses, a man who was fortunate enough to grow up in Pharaoh's palace, was brought up and educated as an Egyptian. Moses had a comfortable life growing up. However, when he became an adult and witnessed the oppression of his own people, his righteous anger at the injustice rose up. His anger flares up out of control, and he kills an Egyptian one day who was beating a Hebrew slave. Moses has to flee from Egypt and spends forty years tending sheep in Midian.

Stephen, perhaps the most well-known Christian martyr of the Bible, says in Acts 7:25 (NIV), "Moses thought that his own people would realize that God was using him to rescue them, but they did not."

What's so fascinating about the story of Moses is Moses wanted to use his position of authority in Egypt, being raised by Pharaoh's daughter, to deliver his own people. His intentions at age 40 were very noble. I believe when God saw this He was not disappointed with Moses for wanting to take action when he saw his Hebrew brother being beaten by a harsh Egyptian. The problem wasn't Moses' desire to see His people delivered from Egypt; the problem was Moses was trying to take the matter into his own hands. How many times in life, especially if you are a parent, do you see a problem then try to fix it in your own strength?

Your child is off course so you lose your cool and start to yell. At work, your boss is being unfair so you bad mouth them to all your co-workers; or at church, prayer time turns into gossip instead of lifting each other up. The key to seeing the problem resolved is by getting out of the flesh. The flesh nature and the Spirit are in opposition to one another. We must deny our fleshly nature daily and follow Christ. Moses had to learn this the hard way. He spent forty years with Jethro tending sheep before God appeared to him with the answer in a burning bush.

The burning bush was God's response to Moses desiring justice for his people. That response took four decades! How long are we willing to wait in order to see God's promises come to pass? Many times the size of the dream can determine how long we must wait in order to see the fruition of it. Moses desired freedom for an entire nation of people. He had a big dream in his heart. Moses' desire for freedom of his people could be compared to a modern-day Martin Luther King Jr. The Egyptians viewed the Hebrews as less than. Martin Luther King saw the injustices of millions of people simply because they had a different skin color.

Setting people free from oppression and from their oppressors is God's business. It's what He does best. Often, the Lord will choose the most humble individuals to use in order to bring great deliverance for a people group. The Bible says in Numbers 12:3 (NLT), "Now Moses was very humble—more humble than any other person on earth." God chose Moses because of his humility. Likewise, I believe God used Martin Luther King because he was willing to lay his own life down in order to advance civil rights for the African American community. In 1968, he paid the ultimate price of assassination for speaking up and taking nonviolent action against a great evil. However, his life and his legacy have impacted millions upon millions of people around the world forever because of his selflessness as an American minister and spokesman for racial inequality.

When the Lord saw Israel in slavery, His eagle eyes watched in fury as a pagan people group treated the children of Israel harshly. Deuteronomy 32:11 (NASB95) says, "Like an eagle that stirs up its nest, that hovers over its young, He spread His wings and caught them, He carried them on His pinions." In the animal kingdom, the eagle eye is among the strongest in the world. An eagle's eyesight is 4 to 8 times stronger than that of the human eye. Eagles can spot their prey 2 miles away. Even though the eagle might weigh 10 pounds, their eyes are about the same size as a human.

When the Scriptures say God keeps Israel as the apple of His eye, then compares Himself to the majestic eagle with super strong eyesight, He means He is like a hovercraft over the Hebrew people. Nothing escapes His notice concerning the tribe of Israel. Not long ago I was driving home from work, when I began to have a vision. The following Sunday I was to preach on the double portion anointing of Elijah, and one of the examples God gave me to share with the congregation was the way of an eagle with her young. As I drove, I began to see an eagle's nest on my head. The vision was so real I could almost feel the nest as I drove!

At first I was a little alarmed, as I thought maybe I was under a spiritual attack. Then when I realized it was the Lord showing me a revelation (and I stopped rebuking the devil!), the Lord began to show me the eggs hatching baby eaglets. The Holy Spirit told me the eggs represented my dreams and creative ideas, that those ideas were coming to life and being birthed. As I pondered the vision, I went home and researched a little more on eaglets. Eagle eggs incubate for about 35 days, a little over a month. Then, once the eggs hatch, the eaglets are in the nest for another 10 to 12 weeks until they learn to fly.

In the same way, there is a process to seeing our dreams come to pass. There are creative ideas and dreams in your heart that the Holy Spirit will stir up. Those ideas must incubate under the protection and the provision of the Lord. Then, when it's the right time, the things you are praying about and believing for will begin to hatch. After the birth, there is another process that must take place. You must learn to fly. You must learn how to navigate the dream or vision that has begun to see new life. When Moses encountered the Lord at the burning bush, his egg full of freedom for his people began to hatch. However, God did not just set Israel free in 24 hours. Moses had to go back and tell Pharaoh to let God's people go.

God sent plague after plague to display His awesome and terrifying glory to the entire world. By the time Israel made it out to the wilderness, everyone knew who the God of Israel was. Even Rahab, a harlot from Jericho, knew who the God of Israel was. She says in Joshua 2:9-11 (NIV), "I know that the LORD has given you this land and that a great fear of you has fallen on us, so that all who live in this country are melting in fear because of you. We have heard how the LORD dried up the water of the Red Sea for you when you came out of Egypt, and what you did to Sihon and Og, the two kings of the Amorites east of the Jordan, whom you completely destroyed. When we heard of it, our hearts melted in fear and everyone's courage failed because of you, for the LORD your God is God in heaven above and on the earth below."

God intentionally waited before setting the Hebrew people free from Egypt. However, when the time came for their deliverance, God did it in a way the whole earth knew about it. There was no news media to speak of during those days. However, word traveled fast about Israel and the ten plagues God brought upon Pharaoh and his kingdom. During the time of Israel's exodus, there were many pagan gods in the surrounding nations. These pagan nations practiced horrible rituals that were abhorrent to the Lord - everything from sacrificing their own children to false gods in fire to worshipping carved images.

Deuteronomy 32:12 (NASB95) tells us, "The LORD alone guided him, and there was no foreign god with him." In a land full of false gods and foreign idols, the Lord chose the descendants of Jacob to be His own people group.

The prophet Isaiah declares in Isaiah 43:1-2 (NIV), "But now, this is what the LORD says-- He who created you, Jacob, He who formed you, Israel: 'Do not fear, for I have redeemed you; I have summoned you by name; you are Mine. When you pass through the waters, I will be with you; and when you pass through the rivers, they will not sweep over you. When you walk through the fire, you will not be burned; the flames will not set you ablaze.'" As we look at and marvel at the modern state of Israel as believers, it is important to remember that it is the Lord who formed Israel.

God created the Jewish state of Israel for His own purposes. Like a potter who never takes his eyes off the spinning clay while he is sculpting its shape and form, so God's eyes have never left the land of Israel. Furthermore, God's promise to Israel is a promise to His church. The Lord has redeemed you. The God of Israel has called you by name. He says, "You are Mine! Do not fear!" When I first visited New York City, I felt overwhelmed. There was so much to see. In New York, you see it all. It is like modern day Babylon. All that the world has to offer is in a great city like New York.

I remember one day while spending time touring Manhattan the Lord telling me to stay away from certain places. I don't believe it was because God was trying to keep something good from me, but rather, He was keeping something from me for my good. There are spiritual threats in this world that we must be protected from as God's children. I have seen young men and women who have grown up in the church move to big cities or become so "educated" that they fall away from the Truth. The Apostle Paul, who saw all the glory of Rome and the best the world had to offer at the time, warns us in Romans 1:21-22 (NASB95) saying, "For even though they knew God, they did not honor Him as God or give thanks, but they became futile in their speculations, and their foolish heart was darkened. Professing to be wise, they became fools."

Simply put: The wisdom of this world will make you dumb in the things of God. God and the world are moving in opposite directions. As the apple of God's eye, you are not going to be allowed by the Holy Spirit to live a life that is in opposition to God's Word. The same is true for Israel. God is not going to allow the Holy Land to be mocked. Those who are standing against her will fall. I remember one day while I was living in New York visiting one of the towers in the Financial District. As I sat in the lobby area near a Starbucks drinking coffee, I began to read my Bible. I started reading the book of Romans. Almost an hour later I had read through the entire book! I don't know what got into me that day, but I remember taking in the Biblical texts in a fresh new way.

The grandeur and power of Rome during Paul's day resembles that of modern day New York. The issues Paul addressed in the book of Romans then still apply today. What's also fascinating is how deeply interwoven the Jewish community in New York is with the nation of Israel. If nearly half of the Jewish people in the world live in Israel and the other half live in the United States - that is, primarily New York City and Los Angeles - then these places must be very important in God's eyes. These are the literal descendants of Jacob, and therefore, places of great power during these end times.

The Bible tells us that in the last days all of Israel will be saved (see Romans 11:26). Deuteronomy 32:13 (KJV) tells us, "He made him [Israel, the

Jewish people] ride on the high places of the earth, that he might eat the increase of the fields; and He made him to suck honey out of the rock, and oil out of the flinty rock." God has mandated a powerful blessing on Israel and the Jewish people. If you have ever wondered why so many brilliant people that have impacted our world come from the Jewish people group, wonder no more! Think of geniuses like Albert Einstein (a physicist), Milton Friedman (an economist), and Emma Lazarus (the author and poet who wrote, "Give me your tired, your poor, your huddled masses yearning to be free," which is prominently displayed on the Statue of Liberty).

Only a little over 900 Nobel Prizes have been awarded to outstanding men and women over the past century. Over 20% of those awards have gone to Jewish people even though the Jewish population accounts for less than 0.2% of the whole world's population. The Song of Moses testifies to the blessing that has been sung of the Hebrew people over the ages. Indeed, the Lord has made His people to "ride on the high places of the earth". I have noticed in my travels, when I am in a place of great influence like Washington DC, New York City, or Los Angeles, there are always influential Jewish people who are leading the way nearby. Being the great Zionist I am, I often tear up when I see the Jewish people thriving and taking positions of leadership.

After witnessing the remains of the concentration camps and watching current day news reports with sorely misled anti-Semites chanting "Death to Israel!" in their streets, I am filled with a sense of pride for the Jewish people. Even though I do not hold all the same beliefs as some Jewish people, I admire them knowing what God has declared over them as the children of Abraham, Isaac, and Jacob. There is an irrevocable, commanded blessing on the Jewish people from the Lord. He is not sitting back watching His people go to hell in a handbasket. While a partial hardening has happened among the Jewish people in these last days (see Romans 11:25), God has not forgotten His promises to their Jewish ancestors that we read about in the Scriptures.

Not long ago I had a LASIK surgery operation performed on my eyes. Ironically, I had just preached a sermon not many days before the surgery entitled "Seeing in the Spirit", where I talked about seeing things through spiritually correct vision. Jesus tells us in Matthew 6:22-23 (NKJV), "The lamp of the body is the eye. If therefore your eye is good, your whole body will be full of light. But if your eye is bad, your whole body will be full of darkness. If therefore the light that is in you is darkness, how great is that darkness!" Seeing things in life from God's Word and from His perspective is how we see clearly and judge accurately. However, there are many today who think they are seeing clearly, but really they are being misled.

Before I had LASIK, I needed either contacts or glasses in order to see clearly far away. Up close I could see better, but I still needed glasses or contacts if I wanted to see what was in front of me. Without something to correct my vision (in this case, the glasses or contacts over my eyes), I could not see clearly what was up ahead. When the doctor performed LASIK on my eyes, he cut a flap in the cornea of my eye. Then he used a laser to reshape my cornea so that it refracts light perfectly onto the retina at the back of my eye. Without light being perfectly bent, or refracted, at the cornea to the retina, my vision would be blurry.

The retina has one primary purpose in the eye. Its job is to convert the light that the eye has captured into electric signals the brain can then process. The retina catches and absorbs the light coming through your pupil and lens. The pupil is the part of the eye that allows light to enter your eye so it can be focused onto the retina in order to begin the process of sight. Whatever light the eye takes in is ultimately processed by the brain and causes us to have eyesight. If Jesus is our Light, and He is the light we are taking in, then we are going to be able to see correctly in the Spirit. If our light is something else other than Jesus Christ, we are not taking any light in at all and cannot see anything in the Spirit.

Maybe today you are a Christian, but like me, your eyesight needs some modifying. I believe God is the ultimate LASIK surgeon. He can correct anyone's vision who comes to Him! The Apostle James tells us in James 1:5 (NIV), "If any of you lacks wisdom, you should ask God, Who gives generously to all without finding fault, and it will be given to you." With everything that is going on in the world today, we need more wisdom from above than ever before to adapt to and adjust to the culture. How we build God's Kingdom now is going to have a great impact on the generations to come. Are we teaching our children to love and appreciate Israel's place in the world? Are we teaching our grandchildren that Israel is the apple of God's eye?

The world is not always going to tolerate the existence of Israel as a Jewish state. The good news is God is greater than this world. There is no kingdom or people group who can overthrow God's plans for Israel and the Jewish people. With many people in the world who do not believe Israel has the right to exist, there is going to be great opposition for anyone who stands with Israel. Not long ago I heard an expression on

TV, and it was one I really liked, as it rang great truth for every believer. The expression was "I would rather stand with God and be judged by the world, than stand with the world and be judged by God." The world is not going to support you if you stand with Israel.

The world is against Israel, because the world is under the influence of deception. The Apostle Paul explains in 2 Thessalonians 2:9-12 (ESV) saying, "The coming of the lawless one is by the activity of Satan with all power and false signs and wonders, and with all wicked deception for those who are perishing, because they refused to love the truth and so be saved. Therefore God sends them a strong delusion, so that they may believe what is false, in order that all may be condemned who did not believe the truth but had pleasure in unrighteousness." Brothers and sisters, this strong delusion from the Lord has already been sent out into the world. Those who have rejected the gospel message are under its power.

The false narrative that Israel has no right to exist is a lie from the enemy, and one that the Church must stand against. Israel is the apple of God's eye, and therefore should be the apple of our eyes also. Whatever is of interest to God should be of interest to us. The wellbeing of Israel is the wellbeing of the entire world. Romans 11:12 (NIV) says, "But if their transgression means riches for the world, and their loss means riches for the Gentiles, how much greater riches will their full inclusion bring!" When Israel is accepted by the Church and fully accepts the gospel message of Christ's salvation, the world is going to explode with a whole new level of blessings we have never seen before!

If you long to see revival in the world, you must pray for Israel. Israel is where the gospel message began, and it is where the end of this age will conclude. It is no wonder the devil works so hard to keep people from praying for and defending Israel. Israel is a huge threat to his demonic kingdom that will one day perish for eternity. In the culture and through political agendas, the enemy is promoting biases against Israel and against the Jews. When God gave Abraham the blessing, the devil has never stopped trying to destroy his children. 1 Peter 5:8 (NIV) tells us, "Be alert and of sober mind. Your enemy the devil prowls around like a roaring lion looking for someone to devour."

There have been various times in my life when the Lord has called me to take a stand for Israel. One of those times has been when I visited Poland and Israel. During election years, it is most obvious how Christians can stand with Israel. There are clear political policies, platforms, and agendas that are for and against the wellbeing of the Jewish state of Israel. I can tell you that the politicians who are coming against Israel and its rightful heirs are going to suffer the consequences for violating what God has already commanded. We get to choose who we are going to vote for during these election years. I know sometimes it feels like you may be choosing between the lesser of two evils, but God has shown us Israel is at the top of His priority list.

Why is Israel at the top of God's priority list in the voting booth? Because Israel always has been and always will be the apple of His eye. When you vote for leaders who support Israel's right to exist, you are showing a form of expression that resists the devil. The Apostle Peter goes on to say in 1 Peter 5:9 (NASB95), "But resist him (the devil), firm in your faith, knowing that the same experiences of suffering are being accomplished by your brethren who are in the world." Anyone who stands with and supports Israel is going to be criticized for it. Some may even be physically attacked for it, as we have seen this happen in different pro-Israel ministries around the world.

The good news today is God is greater than the enemy. He is the Lion of Judah. The devil is a coward in the presence of our King! The intelligent of this world are no match for our God and the plans He has ordained. Nowadays, people have become so "enlightened" by worldly "facts" that they have no use for the Scriptures. The Bible is seen as old, outdated, and irrelevant. The Apostle Paul dealt with the same type of people during his day too. He tells the church in 1 Corinthians 3:18-20 (NLT), "Stop deceiving yourselves. If you think you are wise by this world's standards, you need to become a fool to be truly wise. For the wisdom of this world is foolishness to God. As the Scriptures say, 'He traps the wise in the snare of their own cleverness.' And again, 'The LORD knows the thoughts of the wise; he knows they are worthless.'"

Again, Jesus had issues with the "intelligent" during His day. He says in Luke 10:21 (NLT), "At that same time Jesus was filled with the joy of the Holy Spirit, and He said, 'O Father, Lord of heaven and earth, thank You for hiding these things from those who think themselves wise and clever, and for revealing them to the childlike. Yes, Father, it pleased You to do it this way." Those who are childlike are meek. They are humble. They believe what God said is true, even when they don't fully understand it. In the coming days, more and more countries and businesses around the world will try to raise themselves against Israel and the Holy Land.

The reason is because they are of the world. The world is under a deluding influence. 1 John 5:19 (NIV) tells us, "We know that we are children of God, and that the whole world is under the control of the evil one." Again, the devil hates Israel. God has a covenant with Israel, the Jewish people, and the land where Israel sits. Some even within the church have been misled by believing that when Jesus came, somehow that covenant was nullified. While we have been redeemed out from under the curse of the Law (because of sin), this did not change God's covenant with the Jewish people and the land He promised to them.

God tells Abraham in Genesis 13:15 (NASB95), "For all the land which you see, I will give it to you and to your descendants forever." For those who say Jesus fulfilled the Law (and He certainly did! See Matthew 5:17) and therefore the Holy Land no longer belongs to the Jewish people are forgetting one thing: The promise made to Abraham happened long before the Law of Moses was ever instituted. This promise is not one that can be nullified or revoked. The Apostle Paul rebuked the early church for becoming arrogant towards Israel and the Jewish people for thinking they had somehow replaced the Jewish people as God's people.

Those who are not Jewish have been grafted into the Jewish olive tree. The Jews who were unbelieving were cut off, but God's promise to Abraham never changed. The land God says belongs to Abraham's descendants belongs to them forever and ever. I have also heard it argued that Israel and the Jewish people are "oppressing" the Palestinians who were "already there". The problem with this is not the Palestinian people. The problem is their unbelief. There are non-Jewish Palestinians who love the Lord. Because they have accepted Christ, they know who the land belongs to (and it's not the Palestinian Authority).

So what is the solution to the conflict we see in the Middle East? It's the same answer for the entire world: Jesus Christ. When people accept Jesus Christ, they accept Him as the Word of God. The Word says the deed to the land ordained by Almighty God says, "Property of Israel and the Jewish people." This does not mean a foreigner cannot dwell in Israel. It does mean the hatred that Islam teaches would be dissolved. Islam is the second largest religion in the world (second to Christianity). That makes it the world's largest false religion, and Satan's biggest weapon.

One of our biggest prayers should be salvation for those born into Islam. It is not the fault of those who are born into and raised to believe in the Muslim faith. As a matter of fact, it could be the church is not praying enough for our enemies. We are not praying enough for the Muslims who have been raised to hate infidels. The Koran is filled with the false prophecies and erroneous teachings of Muhammad. Only Jesus can set this people group free! Whenever I engage with other Muslims (usually via the internet), I tell them I am praying Jesus opens their eyes. I also tell them Jesus was more than a prophet. He is the Son of God, and their eternal Savior!

Muslims believe Jesus was a prophet, which He was. However, they do not confess Him to be the Son of God. The problem is no one can go to Heaven or be saved without this confession and acceptance. Even the Jewish people, whom I love dearly, must accept Jesus Christ as their personal Lord and Savior. To reject this is the ultimate and the only unforgivable sin. Jesus warns us in Matthew 12:31-32 (NASB95), saying,

"Therefore I say to you, any sin and blasphemy shall be forgiven people, but blasphemy against the Spirit shall not be forgiven. Whoever speaks a word against the Son of Man, it shall be forgiven him; but whoever speaks against the Holy Spirit, it shall not be forgiven him, either in this age or in the age to come."

God is merciful. He is not willing that anyone should perish! However, He has given everyone freewill. When a person hears the Word of God being preached and taught, they get to choose whether or not they believe what is being said. We see this all the time now in the news and on social media. Not long ago I saw a Christian political leader who believes God created the heavens and the earth in six literal days being viciously slammed by daytime TV show hosts, who believe in evolution and other false doctrines of the world. These TV hosts even called this political leader schizophrenic for praying out loud to God.

The Lord warned us that the world will not tolerate His Word, nor those who believe and follow it. Jesus tells us in John 15:18 (NLT), "If the world hates you, remember that it hated Me first." There are many in the world who hate Israel and don't even really know why. The reason they despise Israel is because they are not walking in the light. Their eyes must be opened by the Spirit of God. Jesus says in John 6:44-47 (NIV), "No one can come to Me unless the Father who sent Me draws them, and I will raise them up at the last day. It is written in the Prophets: 'They will all be taught by God.' Everyone who has heard the Father and learned from Him comes to Me. No one has seen the Father except the One who is from God; only He has seen the Father. Very truly I tell you, the one who believes has eternal life."

The hypocrisy of the scribes and Pharisees blinded them from seeing Jesus as the fulfillment of Messianic prophecy. Their own knowledge and pride caused them to miss the divine visitation of Jesus in their time. The Lord rebuked them for their hypocrisy many times throughout the gospels. He says in Matthew 7:3-5 (NIV), "Why do you look at the speck of sawdust in your brother's eye and pay no attention to the plank in your own eye? How can you say to your brother, 'Let me take the speck out of your eye,' when all the time there is a plank in your own eye? You hypocrite, first take the plank out of your own eye, and then you will see clearly to remove the speck from your brother's eye.'"

I truly believe there were some Pharisees, like Saul who became the Apostle Paul, who later received the gospel message of salvation through Jesus. Many others went to the grave hardened of heart and deceived. It is because of their rejection that God caused Jerusalem to be torn down and the Jewish people to be scattered. However, it is important to note that God's covenant with them was not nullified as some within the church have mistakenly assumed. The partial hardening of hearts is temporary (see Romans 11:25). To reject the Messiah, who is the One all of the Law and the Prophets testified about (see Luke 24:27), was the grave mistake of Israel.

The good news is God's not finished with Israel. In these last days, I believe He has just begun! As we see more technologies pour out of Israel, the world is going to witness things never seen before. Modern-day Israel is still the apple of God's eye. It is a nation to behold and to marvel. The hand of God covers Israel as it is the beacon of freedom in the Middle East. The divine spirit of wisdom and revelation is at work in the people of Israel. To bless the land of Israel is to invoke a blessing upon yourself. How much more of a blessing is it to dwell and abide in this nation set apart from the entire world!

When I visited Israel, I had visions I had never seen before. Around every corner and seemingly every rock I saw, there was a story, or testimony, to the presence of God. Landmarks throughout the nation are a testament to all of the stories we read about in the Scriptures. The God of Israel is real! Nowhere else on earth can His divine fingerprints be seen more clearly. Israel was never meant to just be a blessing for the Jewish people exclusively. Israel is meant to be seen and experienced by the entire world.

When you look at a world map, and you look at Israel and where it sits, it is tiny! This small piece of land sits right in the midst of Arab lands. The prophet Isaiah declares in Isaiah 60:22 (NLT), "The smallest family will become a thousand people, and the tiniest group will become a mighty nation. At the right time, I, the LORD, will make it happen." God did not choose Israel because it was the strongest country or the largest people group. He actually did just the opposite. He chose the few. He chose Abraham, Isaac, and Jacob. When Abraham stared at the stars at night, he would sit and count. There were too many to be numbered (see Genesis 15:5).

As Israel began to form many years ago, God's eye saw to it that each generation carried forward His Word to the next generation. Even during periods of darkness, when the people were not seeking Him, He would stir up prophets and leaders to draw the people back to Himself. From the beginning God's desire has been to bring the hope of salvation to the world through Israel and the promised Messiah. Jesus is the fulfillment of this Old Testament prophecy. Isaiah 62:1-3 (NKJV) tells us, "For Zion's sake I will not hold My peace, and for Jerusalem's sake I will not rest, until her righteousness goes forth as brightness, and her salvation as a lamp that burns. The Gentiles shall see your righteousness, and all kings your glory. You shall be called by a new name, which the mouth of the LORD will name. You shall also be a crown of glory in the hand of the LORD, and a royal diadem in the hand of your God."

The message of salvation was launched from a cross at Golgotha outside the old city gates of Jerusalem. Indeed, righteousness has gone forth into all the world through Christ and the sufferings He endured for our sake. As children of God, redeemed by the King of the Jews, we are watchmen on the walls of Jerusalem today. Isaiah 62:6-7 (NIV) declares, "I have posted watchmen on your walls, Jerusalem; they will never be silent day or night. You who call on the LORD, give yourselves no rest, and give Him no rest till He establishes Jerusalem and makes her the praise of the earth." The whole world is watching Jerusalem right now.

The literal and spiritual war surrounding Jerusalem is intensifying. There is still conflict over who the city of Jerusalem belongs to. We know it belongs to the Jewish people. We know it belongs to the descendants of Abraham. Jerusalem was always intended to be governed by the Jewish people. God has mandated it, and we will not see it come to fruition if the watchmen on the wall do not pray continually for her peace, prosperity, and restoration. God has made an eternal and unconditional covenant with the Jews. Genesis 15:18 (NASB95) says, "On that day the LORD made a covenant with Abram, saying, 'To your descendants I have given this land.'"

When Israel's walls were being rebuilt after the Jews' exile to Babylon for 70 years, the Lord called His people back to the Homeland. During this return, God commissioned leaders like Nehemiah and Ezra to rebuild the walls of Jerusalem - thus, re-establishing the capital of Judah. Just like today, the opposition then for Israel's right to exist was strong. The neighbors of Israel taunted Nehemiah and the workers, even sending false reports back to the king of Babylon, trying to keep them from rebuilding the walls of Jerusalem.

However, the Lord sent His holy angels to guard Jerusalem while the walls were being rebuilt. Zechariah 2:2-5 (NLT) says, "'Where are you going?' I asked. The angel replied, 'I am going to measure Jerusalem, to see how wide and how long it is.' Then the angel who was with me went to meet a second angel who was coming toward him. The other angel said, 'Hurry, and say to that young man, 'Jerusalem will someday be so full of people and livestock that there won't be room enough for everyone! Many will live outside the city walls. Then I, myself, will be a protective wall of fire around Jerusalem, says the LORD. And I will be the glory inside the city!'"

The vision Zechariah had from the Lord was powerful during his day. The people of Israel had lost everything. The temple was destroyed and in ruins; the city walls were torn down. Besides being in exile for decades, the people were deeply discouraged and beat down from living in Babylon away from home. However, God never forgot His covenant with the Hebrew people. He says in Zechariah 2:7-10 (ESV), "Up! Escape to Zion, you who dwell with the daughter of Babylon. For thus said the LORD of hosts, after His glory sent me to the nations who plundered you, for he who touches you touches the apple of His eye: Behold, I will shake My hand over them, and they shall become plunder for those who served them. Then you will know that the LORD of hosts has sent me. Sing and rejoice, O daughter of Zion, for behold, I come and I will dwell in your midst, declares the LORD."

Despite Israel and Judah's rebellion against God, despite their exile to Babylon as punishment, despite all of their shortcomings, God still was merciful with the Jewish people. He did not allow Babylon to trample on the Hebrew people forever. There was a set time for exile and punishment, and there was a set time for God's people to return to the Jewish Homeland. Because the Babylonians were arrogant and did not honor God but thought it was their own strength that brought them victory, the Lord ended up bringing their kingdom to an end. In the same way, whenever we go through a hardship or a trial, God is keeping the records. He will not allow you to suffer and endure persecution forever. He has a set time for allowing the injustice, but He also has a set time for bringing judgment and justice to the situation.

Just like the Jews are the apple of God's eye, all of the Church today is the apple of God's eye. From the beginning God had a plan to reconcile the entire world to Himself through the Jewish people and the Messiah that came from them. The next two verses in Zechariah are so important, as it applies to the entire world and not just the Jews coming back from exile. Zechariah 2:11-12 (ESV) says, "And many nations shall join themselves to the LORD in that day, and shall be My people. And I will dwell in your midst, and you shall know that the LORD of hosts has sent Me to you. And the LORD will inherit Judah as his portion in the holy land, and will again choose Jerusalem." It is so important to remember how intertwined the

Old Testament and New Testament are in our Bibles.

God already knew the new covenant that was to come before He ever gave the old covenant. People from all nations are now joined to the Lord and to the Holy Land through the precious blood of Jesus. We are all one family of God through the Son of God. 1 Peter 1:18-20 (NIV) tells us, "For you know that it was not with perishable things such as silver or gold that you were redeemed from the empty way of life handed down to you from your ancestors, but with the precious blood of Christ, a lamb without blemish or defect. He was chosen before the creation of the world, but was revealed in these last times for your sake." Notice, the Scriptures say Jesus was foreknown and chosen before anything was ever created. Before Genesis 1:1, Jesus was already in existence.

The temple of God was established in Jerusalem. It was in the temple courts that Jesus often taught. Jerusalem was, is, and will always be the apple of God's eye. Under the new covenant, the veil to the old temple was torn in half as Jesus gave His final breath on the cross, signifying the fulfillment of the Law and required sacrifice needed to permanently make atonement for sin. Because we house the Holy Spirit, we are the new temple of God (see 1 Corinthians 6:19). As Spirit-filled believers, one of our callings is to be the watchmen on the walls of Jerusalem. We are called to stand guard for the wellbeing of Jerusalem and her inhabitants. We are called to pray for the shalom peace of God to watch over and protect Israel.

Through Christ, we are attached to the welfare of Israel. Our spiritual heritage and inheritance has come through Christ and the Jewish people. Through Christ, we are all God's children. Psalm 17:7-9 (NIV) says, "Show me the wonders of Your great love, You who save by Your right hand those who take refuge in You from their foes. Keep me as the apple of Your eye; hide me in the shadow of Your wings from the wicked who are out to destroy me, from my mortal enemies who surround me." Know today that God is keeping you as the apple of His eye. Just as God watches over Israel, so He watches over you and me. You and I have inherited the blessings given to the Jewish people. Jesus' blood has made a way for all people from every tribe, nation, and tongue to join in the blessings given to the Hebrew people.

Next time you see the word "Israel" and the blessing that follows it in the Scriptures, you can be sure that blessing now goes not only to the nation of Israel, but also to those who are under the blood of Jesus Christ. Numbers 24:9 (NLT) tells us, "Like a lion, Israel crouches and lies down; like a lioness, who dares to arouse her? Blessed is everyone who blesses you, O Israel, and cursed is everyone who curses you." Whenever you read this, know that you are like a lion of God in the spiritual sense. Those who bless you are going to be blessed, because you are serving the Living God. Those who curse you are only bringing a curse upon themselves. When the enemy tries to get you stirred up, he's messing with the wrong son, the wrong daughter, of God!

We are the children of Israel in Jesus' name. We are grafted into all of the promises God has made to Abraham, Isaac, Jacob, and their descendants through Christ (see 2 Corinthians 1:20). Implanted deep inside of you is a Jewish seed. This seed is always growing, as God causes it to grow (1 Corinthians 3:6). This seed is eternal life (1 Peter 1:23). It is the Word of God (James 1:21). The dividing wall that separated Israel and the Jews from the rest of the world is now broken down (Ephesians 2:14). We are all now one people group through the Son of God! As such, we should celebrate the miraculous rebirth of Israel. We should praise the Lord that He is restoring the land back to its intended recipients after all these years.

As children of God, we should value God and His Word, just as He values us. King Solomon says in Proverbs 7:1-2 (NIV), "My son, keep my words and store up my commands within you. Keep my commands and you will live; guard my teachings as the apple of your eye." When you make God and His Word the apple of your eye, you are keeping the Scriptures and teachings of God at the forefront of your mind. You are intentional about spending time with God every single day. We should be very protective of the Word of God. It is the Word we must hold on to tightly.

Also, we should keep Israel on the forefront of our minds and in our hearts. If Israel is still the apple of God's eye, shouldn't it be of great concern to the Church and God's people around the world also? Is it not the Church God intends to use in these last days to help solidify Israel's rightful place in the Middle East? If the Church does not stand up for Israel, God has ways of passing over even Christians and bringing about His plans. The good news is anyone who wants to participate in being a builder of the walls of Jerusalem (allegorically speaking) is also going to eat the fruits and the blessings thereof.

Psalm 51:18 (NIV) tells us, "May it please You to prosper Zion, to build up the walls of Jerusalem." Today I believe God is calling you to be a part of His divine plans to bless and prosper Israel. There is a commanded blessing on you as you choose to obey God's Word. God promises to pour out His favor on you for looking to the needs of Israel. The Lord tells His people in Deuteronomy 7:13-14 (NIV), "He will love you and bless you and increase your numbers. He will bless the fruit of your womb, the crops of your land--your grain, new wine and olive oil--the calves of your herds and the lambs of your flocks in the land He swore to your ancestors to give you. You will be blessed more than any other people; none of your men or women will be childless, nor will any of your livestock be without young."

I believe today this promised blessing to the Jewish people is also for you. Israel is the apple of God's eye. You are the apple of God's eye. All who belong to Christ are the apple of God's eye. Collectively, we are the family of God. Just as God causes Israel and the Jewish people to stand out from the crowd, God wants to cause you to stand out for His glory. We are all brothers and sisters in Christ. The gospel message (that is, the Good News) is now anyone can walk in the blessings and favor of God! The Apostle Paul tells the Church at Rome in Romans 1:16 (NIV), "For I am not ashamed of the gospel, because it is the power of God that brings salvation to everyone who believes: first to the Jew, then to the Gentile."

Jesus preached the gospel to the Jews first. Then, He chose Paul to preach the gospel to the Gentiles. Paul says in Romans 15:8-12 (NLT), "Remember that Christ came as a servant to the Jews to show that God is true to the promises He made to their ancestors. He also came so that the Gentiles might give glory to God for His mercies to them. That is what the psalmist meant when he wrote: 'For this, I will praise You among the Gentiles; I will sing praises to Your name.' And in another place it is written, 'Rejoice with His people, you Gentiles.' And yet again, 'Praise the LORD, all you Gentiles. Praise Him, all you people of the earth.' And in another place

Isaiah said, 'The heir to David's throne will come, and He will rule over the Gentiles. They will place their hope on Him.'"

Jesus Christ is the same yesterday, today, and forever. He was born in a manger Jewish. He died on the cross as a Jew. He is King of the Jews. As the Son of God, He is King of the Gentiles as well. He is King over all the earth! Because you have His Spirit living in you, you also have the Jewish spiritual bloodline running through your veins. Israel is the apple of His eye. You carry the Spirit of a true Israelite, and therefore, you too are the apple of God's eye. Give the Lord all praise! He is the King of all Kings and is always worthy of our worship and adoration!

REASON FIVE

Inwardly You are Jewish

"Don't judge a book by its cover." This English idiom holds profound truth in a world that seems to judge everything by looks and outward appearance. This phrase means we should not pass judgment on the value of something or someone based on outward appearances alone. When Jesus ministered on the earth He continually butt heads with the Pharisees and Sadducees over this very issue. Outward appearance was everything to the religious leaders. To them, how things looked externally was far more important than the heart. The religious leaders were so legalistic over the Sabbath day of rest that even Jesus performing a miracle on this particular day of the week offended their hardened hearts.

Jesus calls out their hypocrisy when He tells them in John 7:19-24 (NIV), "'Has not Moses given you the Law? Yet not one of you keeps the Law. Why are you trying to kill Me?' 'You are demon-possessed,' the crowd answered. 'Who is trying to kill You?' Jesus said to them, 'I did one miracle, and you are all amazed. Yet, because Moses gave you circumcision (though actually it did not come from Moses, but from the patriarchs), you circumcise a boy on the Sabbath. Now if a boy can be circumcised on the

Sabbath so that the Law of Moses may not be broken, why are you angry with Me for healing a man's whole body on the Sabbath? Stop judging by mere appearances, but instead judge correctly.'"

Because the Jewish leaders were not right with God on the inside, they incorrectly judged Jesus' works when He demonstrated the power of God during His time of public ministry. Up until Jesus came into the world, the people of God were subject to the Law of Moses. There was no new covenant of grace. There was no permanent forgiveness of sins. There was only temporary atonement of sins made by the high priest of Israel. Instead of seeking God from the heart, many of the religious leaders had become so bound up in self-righteousness that they missed the Son of God when He appeared to them! The Apostle Paul rebukes the Jewish people who sought to be justified by their own merit.

Paul tells the church in Romans 2:25-27 (NCV), "If you follow the Law, your circumcision has meaning. But if you break the Law, it is as if you were never circumcised. People who are not Jews are not circumcised, but if they do what the Law says, it is as if they were circumcised. You Jews have the written Law and circumcision, but you break the Law. So those who are not circumcised in their bodies, but still obey the Law, will show that you are guilty." In other words, just because a Jewish person is circumcised according to the Law that still does not automatically make them right with God. Paul argues it is far better to do what is right, living from the heart, than it is to just merely go by external religious practices. It is more important to live for God from the heart than it is to sit through a church service in order to be seen by others.

The Apostle Paul drives home his point when he says in Romans 2:28-29 (NASB95), "For he is not a Jew who is one outwardly, nor is circumcision that which is outward in the flesh. But he is a Jew who is one inwardly; and circumcision is that which is of the heart, by the Spirit, not by the letter; and his praise is not from men, but from God." Those who are truly Jewish are the ones who live with a heart set on God. Because you are a follower of Christ, inwardly you are Jewish! No matter who your parents are, what your nationality is, or how you were raised, when you received Jesus Christ to be Lord of your life, spiritually speaking, you were circumcised. Your heart has been changed, and you are dedicated to the Lord forever.

Sometimes when I am lying in bed at night praying, I have similar reoccurring visions. One of the visions I've had at various points in my life is me lying on an operating table in front of a heart surgeon. My chest is wide open, and the surgeon is prudently working on my heart. As I lie there, I'm not moving. I'm just being. I'm still. I'm not saying a word. As this vision continues I see it is the Lord who is operating on me. In my spirit I know God is showing me that He is the ultimate heart surgeon. He is the only One who can truly change and mend the heart. This is why when we are praying for someone we care about, we need to leave that person in the hands of God.

We cannot fix anybody. Only God can cause a person's heart to change. King Solomon tells us in Proverbs 21:1-2 (NLT), "The king's heart is like a stream of water directed by the LORD; He guides it wherever He pleases. People may be right in their own eyes, but the LORD examines their heart." The Lord is the Creator of the heart. He can turn it whichever way He so chooses. When the Apostle Paul says that we are circumcised in the heart, he is saying we are in a covenant that is supernaturally bound to the Lord on the inside. External circumcision means nothing when it pertains to following the Lord. It makes you no more or no less one of God's children. Before Christ came, the Jewish people were under the Law of Moses. After Jesus came, He fulfilled the Law as the Messiah. Now we no longer walk according to the letter of the Law but according to Christ's Spirit. Anyone who has given their life to Christ is spiritually Jewish.

Those who do the deeds of someone who is godly are the children of God. Jesus rebukes the Jews by natural birth in the Book of Revelation and encourages those who are truly followers of God when He says in Revelation 3:7-10 (ESV), "And to the angel of the church in Philadelphia write: 'The words of the Holy One, the true One, Who has the key of David, Who opens and no one will shut, Who shuts and no one opens. I know your works. Behold, I have set before you an open door, which no one is able to shut. I know that you have but little power, and yet you have kept My word and have not denied My name. Look, I will force those who belong to Satan's synagogue—those liars who say they are Jews but are not—to come and bow down at your feet. They will acknowledge that you are the ones I love. Because you have kept My word about patient endurance, I will keep you from the hour of trial that is coming on the whole world, to try those who dwell on the earth."

The Scriptures make it clear that only those who keep Jesus' word are the ones that are truly Jews. Whether you have Jewish people in your family lineage or not, we are all brought into God's true Kingdom through the blood of Jesus Christ. The word "Jew" originates from the Hebrew word "Yehudi". Yehudi means "from the kingdom of Judah". Because Jesus is from the tribe of Judah, and He is the eternal King (see 1 Timothy 1:17), anyone who confesses Jesus as Lord now carries His name. In God's eyes we are no longer defined by who our ancestors are. We are defined by who we are in Christ and only in Christ. Otherwise, none of us are made righteous before God.

The good news today is you are the righteousness of God (2 Corinthians 5:21). If you identify as a Christian, then you are identified as belonging to the eternal King of Judah. If you belong to the King of Judah, you are a "Yehudi". You are "from the Kingdom of Judah"! Your citizenship is not based upon where you were born or who your parents are. Your citizenship is based upon what God's Word says. The Bible makes it clear who you are and where you came from. John 1:10-13 (NIV) says, "Jesus was in the world, and though the world was made through Him, the world did not recognize Him. He came to that which was His own [the Jews], but His own did not receive Him. Yet to all who did receive Him, to those who believed in His name [Jesus], He gave the right to become children of God--children born not of natural descent, nor of human decision or a husband's will, but born of God."

Brothers and sisters, you are born and now alive because of God. How you got here and who you came through are secondary to the fact that you are here because God willed it so. The Bible warns us to not subject ourselves to the Old Testament Law according to the flesh. The Law given to the Jewish people cannot make anyone righteous. Only Jesus Christ can pardon sin indefinitely. The Apostle Paul tells the church in Philippians 3:2-3 (NLT), "Watch out for those dogs, those people who do evil, those mutilators who say you must be circumcised to be saved. For we who worship by the Spirit of God are the ones who are truly circumcised. We rely on what Christ Jesus has done for us. We put no confidence in human effort."

The unbelieving Jewish leaders during this time of Paul's writing were teaching that men must be physically circumcised in order to be saved. Paul refutes the teaching, as this would mean salvation could be based upon workings of the Law rather than the free gift of salvation by believing in Jesus. The message of salvation is very simple. All who believe in Jesus Christ as the Son of God shall be saved. Those who have given their lives to Christ are the true "circumcision". These are the ones who are circumcised, or set aside for the Lord, from the inside out.

One of the more modern debates similar to what the religious leaders incorrectly taught about circumcision as a requirement to be saved is the argument that physical water baptism is required to be saved. While water baptism is very important in the new believer's walk with God, it is not the water nor the "dunking" in the water that saves a person. It is an external expression of an internal change of a person's heart. If water baptism is what is required for a person to be saved, then the thief who died on the cross next to Jesus would have never gone to Heaven! (See Luke 23:39-43)

Romans 8:2-4 (ESV) tells us, "For the law of the Spirit of life has set you free in Christ Jesus from the law of sin and death. For God has done what the Law, weakened by the flesh, could not do. By sending His own Son in the likeness of sinful flesh and for sin, He condemned sin in the flesh, in order that the righteous requirement of the Law might be fulfilled in us, who walk not according to the flesh but according to the Spirit." When the

Apostle Paul says the word "Law", he is referring to the Law of Moses. He is referring also to the circumcision requirement within the Law of Moses. Because no one could ever possibly walk perfectly under the Law of Moses, all people fall short of God's righteousness and are worthy of death.

The only one who fulfilled the Law of Moses is Jesus, who is the Son of God (Matthew 5:17). The only way for us to fulfill the Law of Moses is by walking in Christ's Spirit. We must put on the Spirit of Christ (Romans 13:14). To be truly Jewish is to walk in Christ's Spirit. Paul tells us in Romans 8:13-14 (NIV), "For if you live according to the flesh, you will die; but if by the Spirit you put to death the misdeeds of the body, you will live. For those who are led by the Spirit of God are the children of God." Before Jesus ever walked the earth, Moses told the Israelites that one day a Prophet would come that was like himself. He tells the congregation in Deuteronomy 18:15 (NASB95), "The LORD your God will raise up for you a Prophet like me from among you, from your countrymen, you shall listen to Him."

Jesus is the fulfillment of this prophetic word Moses delivered that day. Moses goes on to say in Deuteronomy 18:18-19 (NIV), "I will raise up for them a Prophet like you from among their fellow Israelites, and I will put My words in His mouth. He will tell them everything I command Him. I Myself will call to account anyone who does not listen to My words that the Prophet speaks in My name." When people reject you for believing the Bible and what it says, they are not just rejecting you or the one who is preaching and teaching. They are rejecting God, and God will hold them accountable for it. There are grave consequences for those who will not listen to the truth.

Jesus tells us plainly He is the Prophet Moses was referring to. He says in John 12:49 (NIV), "For I did not speak on My own, but the Father who sent Me commanded Me to say all that I have spoken." When Jesus tells us He is the only way to Heaven (John 14:6) and all other ways lead to destruction (Matthew 7:13), He is speaking only what God the Father told Him to say. Anyone who rejects this statement is going to answer to God for it on the day of judgment. When you speak the Word of God and stand on what the Bible says, the flack and opposition you receive from the world is not really an attack on you. It's an attack on the One who gave you His Word.

People may give you a hard time for following Christ. They may call you names and categorize you as a religious nut, but they cannot change the Truth according to God's Word. God's Word is eternal. It never changes, and God never changes. Malachi 3:6 (NLT) says, "I am the LORD, and I do not change. That is why you descendants of Jacob are not already destroyed." Even during Israel's rebellion, the Lord did not completely destroy the people of Israel because of His promises to their ancestors. The Lord says in 2 Kings 8:19 (ESV), "Yet the LORD was not willing to destroy Judah, for the sake of David His servant, since He promised to give a lamp to him and to his sons forever."

God is true to His word. If His Word says that inwardly you are Jewish, then that makes you Jewish in the sense that you inherit the promises of God, both old and new covenant. This new identity in Christ is why we pray for Israel. Our spiritual ancestry runs deep in the land of Israel. You belong to God's tribe. Jews and Gentiles have become one new group of believers. Through Christ we are all God's children that are joined together in one Spirit. (See Ephesians 2:11-22). Since we now identify as being Jewish on the inside, we ought to take the Scriptures written by Jewish people as part of our own heritage. Anyone who is a follower of Jesus Christ is a true descendant of Abraham.

While the Hebrew people considered themselves Jewish because they practiced the Law of Moses and were biological descendants of Abraham, Jesus set a new standard of living for following God that requires and is based upon faith. The Apostle Paul explains this to the church, saying in Galatians 3:5-9 (NLT), "I ask you again, does God give you the Holy Spirit and work miracles among you because you obey the law? Of course not! It is because you believe the message you heard about Christ. In the same way, 'Abraham believed God, and God counted him as righteous because of his faith.' The real children of Abraham, then, are those who put their faith in God. What's more, the Scriptures looked forward to this time when God would make the Gentiles right in His sight because of their faith. God proclaimed this good news to Abraham long ago when He said, 'All nations will be blessed through you.' So all who put their faith in Christ share the same blessing Abraham received because of his faith."

When God was giving the promise to Abraham, He was already thinking about the entire world. When God chose Israel, it is not as if He had forgotten about the rest of the planet. From the beginning, God had a plan to redeem all of His children from every tribe, tongue, and nation. The blessing Abraham received now belongs to us also. Genesis 15:1 (NASB95) says, "After these things the word of the LORD came to Abram in a vision, saying, 'Do not fear, Abram, I am a shield to you; Your reward shall be very great.'" The good news today is the God of Abraham is a shield to you.

When we go through trials and hardships, God is shielding us just as He shielded Abraham. Many times the Lord protects us, and we don't even realize it. Sometimes a business contract falls through because God can already see down the road that it's a bad deal. It would not help us but actually hinder us from moving forward. I've seen time and time again God remove certain people from my path as I've pursued different ideas and dreams. Looking back I can see where the hand of God was protecting me from something I would not have either been able to handle at the time or that would have actually brought loss instead of gain.

God can see the bigger picture for each of our lives. The Scriptures say in Genesis 24:1 (NASB95), "Now Abraham was old, advanced in age; and the LORD had blessed Abraham in every way." God's desire is to bless you in the same way He blessed Abraham. Abraham was surrounded by God's favor and protection. Abraham found success when he obeyed God and did what was right. Abraham's obedience is what brought God's blessing on his life. Genesis 12:1-2 (NIV) tells us, "The LORD had said to Abram, 'Go from your country, your people and your father's household to the land I will show you. I will make you into a great nation, and I will bless you; I will make your name great, and you will be a blessing.'"

When God called Abraham to leave his home where he was comfortable to start over, it was not an easy move. Abraham had to leave his loved ones. He had to depart from his parents and travel to a new place. I'm sure where he was from had plenty of food, livestock, and physical protection. No doubt Abraham had questions and even a fear of the unknown at the time. In the same way, there are times when God is going to call us out of our comfort zone. He is going to call us to make a radical change. For some of us that means we may be called to physically relocate. It could be starting a new ministry or a new business. It could be seeking help to get free from an addiction or a bad relationship.

The call of God is unique for every believer. No two stories are exactly the same. The key is that we live by faith. Just as Abraham could not see with the physical eye all of his children, grandchildren, and great grandchildren that were to be born to him in the future, he knew by the Spirit of God that one day he would have as many descendants as the stars of heaven. Just as God spoke to Abraham in various ways, I believe God is going to speak to you in ways that you can understand what He is calling you to do. The truly Jewish way of life is to walk by faith in God.

When we believe God, we believe His Word. When we believe the revelation He has given us through the Holy Spirit, we are acting like the children of Abraham. This is what it means to be Jewish inwardly. When I began my ministry of writing back in 2014, I had to form a publishing company with a logo for all my different works. As I considered various logo ideas, I was drawn to a bright and fiery looking logo of the Star of David. I have often been asked about the MLM Publishing logo, as it is in the form of a Jewish star. The reason I chose the Jewish star is because I felt it was important to remember our Jewish roots as Christians.

During my times in Malibu, California, I had frequently attended a Messianic Jewish church pastored by Rabbi Jason Sobel. Rabbi Jason's teachings instilled in me a deeper understanding of how the Old and New Testament are intertwined. His understanding of the original Hebrew texts, the alphanumeric meanings throughout the Scriptures, and the

Jewishness of Jesus the Messiah gave me a deeper revelation of how interconnected the Jews and Gentiles truly are through Christ. Our Savior is Jewish. Our Bibles are written by Jews. Everything about our faith stems from the Jewish people.

When I saw the Star of David, I immediately knew this would be the perfect representation for my ministry. It would serve as a reminder to Christians that our root stems from the original Jewish faith. It also serves to remind us of the importance of Israel. If Christ is Jewish, and His Spirit is what lives in us, then that makes us Jewish through Him. While I am not biologically Jewish, I still identify with Jewish believers as my brothers and sisters in Christ. When anyone receives Christ into their heart, their heart is circumcised. They are set apart for the Lord.

Deuteronomy 30:5-6 (NKJV) says, "Then the LORD your God will bring you to the land which your fathers possessed, and you shall possess it. He will prosper you and multiply you more than your fathers. And the LORD your God will circumcise your heart and the heart of your descendants, to love the LORD your God with all your heart and with all your soul, that you may live." The principle seen here is the generational blessing that is passed down when you choose to honor the Lord with all your heart and soul. When you honor God, the blessings flow to your family. They flow to your children, grandchildren, and great grandchildren.

Not only does the generational blessing pass from one generation to the next, but the blessing actually multiplies. What was once the ceiling of one generation becomes the floor for the next generation to build upon. As the church continues to grow from one generation to the next, I believe

God is going to bring an outpouring of the Holy Spirit in greater and more powerful ways. As the darkness grows darker, so the light grows brighter. We are going to see God's glory displayed in His people like never before in these last days!

Acts 2:17-21 (NIV) tells us, "In the last days, God says, I will pour out my Spirit on all people. Your sons and daughters will prophesy, your young men will see visions, your old men will dream dreams. Even on My servants, both men and women, I will pour out My Spirit in those days, and they will prophesy. I will show wonders in the heavens above and signs on the earth below, blood and fire and billows of smoke. The sun will be turned to darkness and the moon to blood before the coming of the great and glorious day of the Lord. And everyone who calls on the name of the Lord will be saved." More displaying of signs, wonders, and miracles is what is coming for the Church.

The Apostle Peter says in Acts 2:22 (NIV), "Fellow Israelites, listen to this: Jesus of Nazareth was a man accredited by God to you by miracles, wonders and signs, which God did among you through Him, as you yourselves know." The people of Israel witnessed the miracles of Jesus, who was one of their fellow Jewish countrymen. The Apostle Paul's bold statement in Romans 2:29 that a person is not Jewish unless they are one inwardly (making Jewishness attained by the heart and not by nationality or religious law) offended the religious leaders.

The Jews prided themselves on the Law of Moses. However, they were hypocritical in their pursuit of God. In the same way, many within the churches today have replaced a personal relationship with God with a religious spirit. The religious spirit is offended by the Spirit of God. The religious spirit says to carry on with the tradition of man. The religious spirit resists change that is from the Holy Spirit. When Jesus spoke and ministered, the religious spirit held the Jewish leaders in bondage. They clung to their religion instead of to God. They clung to religion and to man-made rules instead of God's heart.

They were so darkened and bound up in the spirit of religion that they could not even acknowledge all of the signs, wonders, and miracles performed by Jesus. How many today are offended when someone speaks of another person being supernaturally healed? How many within the church are offended when someone prophesies, and they don't like what the prophet had to say? The religious spirit has no place in the Body of Christ. We see this hypocritical spirit within the churches, just as during the time of Jesus.

The Scriptures say in John 12:37-40 (NASB95), "But though He had performed so many signs before them, yet they were not believing in Him. This happened so that the word of Isaiah the prophet which he spoke would be fulfilled: 'LORD, WHO HAS BELIEVED OUR REPORT? AND TO WHOM HAS THE ARM OF THE LORD BEEN REVEALED?' For this reason they could not believe, for Isaiah said again, 'HE HAS BLINDED THEIR EYES AND HE HARDENED THEIR HEART, SO THAT THEY WILL NOT SEE WITH THEIR EYES AND UNDERSTAND WITH THEIR HEART, AND BE CONVERTED, AND SO I WILL NOT HEAL THEM.'"

When the Holy Spirit begins to move, people are going to be offended. Just as the religious spirit was alive during the times of Jesus' public ministry, so there are people within the church - even within the church leadership - that are under the influence of the spirit of religion. Many times the spirit of religion comes in because of the fear of what people might think. Instead of fearing and honoring what God says, people fear what others are going to think and say. What if I start to pursue the Lord, and I start experiencing some weird things in the Spirit? What if God calls me to speak prophetically over my friend or family member? Even more radical, what if I start to pray in tongues, and my church doesn't even believe that gift exists? (See 1 Corinthians 14:5)

When the Spirit of God begins to move, the sword of the Spirit (which is God's Word, see Ephesians 6:17) is going to begin to cut and divide. Jesus even said that He came to divide the sheep from the goats (Luke 12:51, Matthew 25:32). Jesus knows all whose hearts are committed to Him. He knows the ones who love the Lord and are of His Kingdom. Our job is not to decide who is the sheep and who is the goat. Our job is to testify and operate to the best of our abilities in what God has called us to do. Remember, Jesus is the lion of the tribe of Judah. He is from the kingdom of Judah. Those who are true descendants of Judah are truly Jewish from the inside out.

Even though many of the Jewish leaders believed in Jesus, their fear of man overcame their faith in God. The Scriptures testify to this in John 12:42-43 (NASB95) which says, "Nevertheless many even of the rulers believed in Him, but because of the Pharisees they were not confessing Him, for fear that they would be put out of the synagogue; for they loved the approval of men rather than the approval of God." If we are going to follow Jesus and seek to obey God's Word, many times we are going to be pushed aside by the world.

When the church begins acting like the culture, there is a major problem with the church. The church is called to be the salt and light of the world. The church is called to be the moral standard of living. Unfortunately, many of the churches have replaced the Spirit of God with religious living. Just like the Jewish leaders attended synagogue every week and learned from the Scriptures, so people attend church every week and hear a message preached. However, when Jesus showed up and demonstrated His power as the Son of God and as being the fulfillment of the Law of Moses and all of the prophets that testified about Him, the religious were either offended, afraid of men, or both.

In the same way, there are many who fear going deeper in the things of God and in experiencing the power of the Holy Spirit, as it might rock the religious boat. Walking in the Spirit could offend certain church doctrines or make others uncomfortable. If Jesus showed up today and demonstrated His power before the churches, I wonder how many would receive Him and how many would be offended. We would like to believe that all would celebrate Him, but I am afraid the same religious spirit that was on the Pharisees then is still in operation today.

The good news is there are many who are truly seeking the Lord. I believe as the end of times draws near, it will become evident who the Spirit-filled believers are and who are merely interested in the approval of men. The Apostle Paul says it is those whose hearts are truly circumcised, or in covenant, with God that are Jewish. Paul rocked the religious boat in the synagogues when he preached salvation to not just the Jews, but to the Gentiles also. He offended them when he said that the promises of God are for all believers and that the Law could not save.

Recently I heard the testimony of a minister who, many years ago, began to be led by the Spirit to speak a prophetic word at the church he worked for. The other leaders did not like him demonstrating this spiritual gift. It offended them. It made them uncomfortable, so one of the pastors asked him to either stop giving prophetic words or to leave. As this minister, whose prophetic ministry is now reaching thousands of people around the world years later, kind of laughed as he told the rest of the story he said all he could say when his fellow minister asked him what he was going to do was, "I must be about my Father's business."

I am sure it had to be hard for this minister to leave his church family because of doing something that was very different to what they were accustomed to. However, this minister said shortly after he left that church his ministry exploded in growth. Maybe today you are praying for a breakthrough or a miracle. Like this minister, you may have to let go of some things and come out of a place before you can see the new level of growth that God desires to give you. Your breakthrough could be the day you get out of the boat and begin to walk by faith into new territory.

Abraham did not know what to expect when God called him away from his father and mother. He did not know what to expect when God asked him to tie his son Isaac to the altar and sacrifice him. All he knew is what God said and that was enough for him to obey. When Abraham is conversing with Abimelech, king of Gerar, he says in Genesis 20:13

(NASB95), "And it came about, when God caused me to wander from my father's house, that I said to her (Sarah), 'This is the kindness which you will show to me: everywhere we go, say of me, "He is my brother."'" The reason Abraham told Sarah to tell everyone they met that she was his brother is because he was afraid. Sarah was both Abraham's half-sister and wife (not uncommon during his day, but obviously is now considered incest!).

Abraham had fear. He was surrounded by powerful kings in a foreign land without the protection of his parents. God called Abraham into a place that was unsafe in the natural world. However, Abraham had God's blessing. He had the promise. Everywhere Abraham went God protected him. He gave Abraham success and victory. In the same way, you are a child of Abraham. You are his descendant by faith. When John the Baptist was ministering and preparing the way for Jesus the Messiah to appear to Israel, he rebuked the religious leaders with harsh severity.

Matthew 3:7-10 (NLT) says, "But when he (John the Baptist) saw many Pharisees and Sadducees coming to watch him baptize, he denounced them. 'You brood of snakes!' he exclaimed. 'Who warned you to flee the coming wrath? Prove by the way you live that you have repented of your sins and turned to God. Don't just say to each other, 'We're safe, for we are descendants of Abraham.' That means nothing, for I tell you, God can create children of Abraham from these very stones. Even now the ax of God's judgment is poised, ready to sever the roots of the trees. Yes, every tree that does not produce good fruit will be chopped down and thrown into the fire.'"

The Jewish leaders thought they were immune from God's judgment and wrath because of their biological birthright as a Jew. They believed that because they could tie their genealogy back to Abraham that made them the righteous ones. John the Baptist goes on to say in the next verse, Matthew 3:11 (NLT), "I baptize with water those who repent of their sins and turn to God. But someone is coming soon who is greater than I am—so much greater that I'm not worthy even to be His slave and carry His sandals. He will baptize you with the Holy Spirit and with fire."

Only those who are born again, that is of the Holy Spirit, are the true children of Abraham. To be truly Jewish means to be a true child of Abraham. It means we have faith like Abraham, even when we may have our doubts or legitimate fears. One of Abraham's greatest traits as a follower of God was he did not waiver at the promise God made to him. Abraham left the "family farm" believing God would give him a land of promise. We see how adamant Abraham was about not returning home but staying in the land God led him to when he commissions his servant to go find his son Isaac a wife back home.

Before Abraham dies in his old age, he tells his servant in Genesis 24:3-4 (NIV), "I want you to swear by the LORD, the God of heaven and the God of earth, that you will not get a wife for my son from the daughters of the Canaanites, among whom I am living, but will go to my country and my own relatives and get a wife for my son Isaac." The servant, who is thinking logically about what if this plan of Abraham's does not work, then replies in Genesis 24:5 (NIV), "What if the woman is unwilling to come back with me to this land? Shall I then take your son back to the country you came from?" The way Abraham then reacts to the servant reveals his faith in

God's promise to inherit the land of Canaan.

Genesis 24:6 (NLT) says, "'No!' Abraham responded. 'Be careful never to take my son there. For the LORD, the God of heaven, who took me from my father's house and my native land, solemnly promised to give this land to my descendants. He will send His angel ahead of you, and He will see to it that you find a wife there for my son.'" As we see Abraham's response, we should consider where Abraham is coming from. It took great courage and faith for Abraham to leave his own country to settle in the land of Canaan. The idea of him sending off his son to go back home, and he then die in his old age, was intolerable to Abraham. Jeopardizing God's promise for Abraham's descendants to inherit the land was not an option.

Like Abraham, sometimes you must defend your blessing. You must be adamant like your father Abraham, stomp your foot, and say, "No! I will not go back. My children will not go back. I will not return to where God had me leave. I am moving forward and advancing into the promises God has given me." Abraham was always moving forward with God. He did not look back. He looked ahead to the promise of God. The Scriptures of the New Testament testify to this. Hebrews 11:8-9 (NIV) tells us, "By faith Abraham, when called to go to a place he would later receive as his inheritance, obeyed and went, even though he did not know where he was going. By faith he made his home in the promised land like a stranger in a foreign country; he lived in tents, as did Isaac and Jacob, who were heirs with him of the same promise."

Abraham was staunch when it came to defending his blessing. He would not budge. He reiterates to his servant not to ever take his son back to his original home, saying in Genesis 24:8 (NLT), "If she is unwilling to come back with you, then you are free from this oath of mine. But under no circumstances are you to take my son there." There is much to learn from the faith of Abraham. He is the father of our faith. We are all his children. We are the descendants of the promise that he clung to so dearly. We are the countless descendants (like the stars of the sky and the sand of the seashore) that Abraham gave up everything for. He was even willing to sacrifice his only son Isaac (who was the promised child), believing that God was able to raise him back up from the dead (Hebrews 11:17-19).

The bosom of Abraham in Heaven is where the poor man Lazarus was carried off to by the angels after he died (see Luke 16:22). Abraham's bosom is a place of eternal comfort. Abraham receives us as his children because we are the children promised to him. He loves us and will be there in Heaven one day to welcome us home. Not all who biologically descended from Abraham are Abraham's children. Not all who are born biologically Jewish are Jewish on the inside. Because you have your faith in Christ, you are spiritually Jewish. Your DNA changes the moment you receive Jesus Christ as your personal Lord and Savior.

Because you are one of Abraham's children, the land of Israel should be of great value to you. You have ties to the land of Israel because of your faith. Today Israel is still the center of history. God's covenant with Abraham and His love for Israel has not been nullified. The land still belongs to Abraham's descendants. Hosea 11:1 (ESV) reminds us of this promise, which says, "When Israel was a child, I loved him, and out of Egypt I called my son." The parallels between the Old and New Testament are astounding. When Hosea says Israel, he is referring to the Jewish people that were delivered from the clutches of Pharaoh and his ensuing army.

In the New Testament, Jesus fulfills this prophecy as a young child when He and His parents are forced to flee to Egypt to escape the fury of King Herod (Matthew 2:13-14). The Scriptures say in Matthew 2:15 (NASB95), "He (Jesus) remained there until the death of Herod. This was to fulfill what had been spoken by the Lord through the prophet: 'Out of Egypt I called My Son.'" In today's world, God is still delivering Israel and the Jewish people from her enemies. No matter how many surrounding nations try to wipe Israel off the map, the Lord continues to cover the land with His hand of protection.

The declarations made over Israel in the Old Testament still apply to today. Moses declares a powerful blessing over the nation of Israel in Deuteronomy 33:27-29 (NIV) saying, "The eternal God is your refuge, and underneath are the everlasting arms. He will drive out your enemies before you, saying, 'Destroy them!' So Israel will live in safety; Jacob will dwell secure in a land of grain and new wine, where the heavens drop dew. Blessed are you, Israel! Who is like you, a people saved by the LORD? He is your shield and helper and your glorious sword. Your enemies will cower before you, and you will tread on their heights."

The Lord takes vengeance on any and all who come against the glorious nation of Israel that we can see with our very own eyes today. On the converse, all who bless Israel will partake of Israel's blessings. The blessings flow from the land of Israel and onto all who support her. The 1940s were a profound time in the history of the world. The 1940s started off in the midst of a world war. Most notable, the Holocaust targeted primarily at the

Jewish people occurred from 1941 to 1945. However, by 1948 Israel was miraculously reborn into a Jewish nation once again.

The 1940s also marked a technology boom in the United States that led to an explosion of wealth creation through the 1950s. What's interesting is the rest of the world did not see the roaring economy like in America until the 1960s. One reason I believe the US flourished before other countries did is because of America's immediate response to both rescuing the Jewish people and helping establish the Jewish state of Israel. When the British Mandate of Palestine expired on May 14, 1948, the Jewish People's Council proclaimed the establishment and independence of the State of Israel. In just eleven short minutes after this bold proclamation, the most powerful nation on earth, the United States of America, recognized Israel under the sitting president Harry Truman.

It is important to note that affluence around the world rose dramatically shortly after Israel became an established political nation once again in 1948. As Christians, this should not be a surprise to us. The whole world has always hinged on what is happening in the Middle East. It is the birthplace and the end zone in God's sovereign plan for His people. The explosion of wealth in the world that has been created since Israel was reestablished as a Jewish state a few decades ago is Biblical. Romans 11:12 (NIV) even tells us, "But if their transgression means riches for the world, and their loss means riches for the Gentiles, how much greater riches will their full inclusion bring!"

I strongly believe the United States has boomed economically in the last century because of her treatment of Israel and the Jewish people. Those who tie themselves to the native olive tree will partake of the rich root of blessings it has to offer. Those who oppose Israel will find themselves at war with the God of Israel. The political and spiritual ties between the nation of Israel and the United States has led to the prosperity of both countries. Psalm 33:8-12 (NASB95) says, "Let all the earth fear the LORD; Let all the inhabitants of the world stand in awe of Him. For He spoke, and it was done; He commanded, and it stood fast. The LORD nullifies the counsel of the nations; He frustrates the plans of the peoples. The plan of the LORD stands forever, The plans of His heart from generation to generation. Blessed is the nation whose God is the LORD, The people whom He has chosen for His own inheritance."

Right now Jesus is seated in Heaven on His throne at the right hand of the Father. He is interceding for us. He is making prayers and petitions for the saints. When Jesus was crucified, His title was written and posted above Him for His "criminal charge". His title was written in Hebrew, Latin, and Greek for all the world to see. What was His title that the world so hated? "Jesus of Nazareth, the King of the Jews". What Pilate had inscribed about Jesus was 100% true. John 19:20 tells us that many of the Jews read the inscription as they passed by outside the gates of the old city.

On Calvary's hill, that is the hill of Golgotha (which means "place of the skull"), where centuries before Abraham had willingly offered up Isaac - his one and only son of promise - to God as a sacrifice before an angel of the Lord stopped him, Jesus bore the sins of the world and the wrath of God upon Himself as God's one and only Son. Jesus underwent crucifixion on this hill of Mount Moriah where centuries before King Solomon had resurrected the first Temple of the Lord. While Satan intended to make a mockery of the King of the Jews, Jesus triumphed over him on the third day when God raised Him from the dead.

The truth is Jesus actually got the last laugh when the devil tried to stop Him. Colossians 2:13-15 (NIV) tells us, "When you were dead in your sins and in the uncircumcision of your flesh, God made you alive with Christ. He forgave us all our sins, having canceled the charge of our legal indebtedness, which stood against us and condemned us; He has taken it away, nailing it to the cross. And having disarmed the powers and authorities, He made a public spectacle of them, triumphing over them by the cross."

Jesus made a public display of our enemies when He died on the Cross and rose from the grave. The devil thought He had won when Jesus hung on the cross. Satan knew Jesus was the Son of God. He knew Jesus was the heir to the throne as King of the Jews. Jesus took back the keys to the grave when death had no power over His sinless body. 2 Corinthians 2:14 (NCV) says, "But thanks be to God, who always leads us as captives in Christ's victory parade. God uses us to spread His knowledge everywhere like a sweet-smelling perfume." There is a party going on right now in Heaven. Angels are cheering and celebrating every single time someone accepts Christ as their Savior.

This King of the Jews is leading us in His victory parade right before the enemy. King David says in Psalm 23:5 (NLT), "You prepare a feast for me in the presence of my enemies. You honor me by anointing my head with oil. My cup overflows with blessings." If you could see yourself right now in the Spirit of God, you would see God's holy angels pouring the oil of

God's goodness on your head. You would see blessings bubbling up from deep within your eternal soul. You are made in God's image.

You are made in the image of God like the King of the Jews. That makes you Jewish on the inside. It means your heart has been circumcised and made tender towards God and His Spirit. Any time you see the Star of David, whether it be on the flag of Israel or on a necklace, remember that star represents your identity in Christ. Jesus is a Jewish man, born from a long line of Jewish descendants. His Jewishness now lives on in you. As the Church learns to identify more and more with this Jewish king, the love we all have for Israel will only continue to grow and grow.

All who align themselves with the Jewish state of Israel are going to see both the blessings of God and the opposition of the world. God's heartbeat is still at Mount Moriah where His Son was crucified. His eyes are still on the hill where Abraham offered his son Isaac on the altar as a firstborn sacrifice. His Spirit still watches over Mount Moriah where King Solomon resurrected the first Temple of God on the earth. Calvary's hill serves as a testimony throughout the ages as to what God has done for us through His beloved Son.

The same demons that tried to hold Jesus down and put Him in the grave forever are trying to withhold Christ's Church from advancing God's Kingdom. The good news today is their efforts are futile. Christ has already made a spectacle of them and continues to do so through you and me. We were made to reign in life. When you overcome a financial challenge, you are making a spectacle of the enemy. When you beat an addiction, you just trampled over the devil. When you start agreeing with what God says, you are destroying the fortresses of darkness. Isaiah 25:12 (NIV) says concerning our enemies, "He will bring down your high fortified walls and lay them low; He will bring them down to the ground, to the very dust."

Right now God is laying low anything that is standing between you and Him. He is removing any obstacles keeping you from becoming who He made you to be. Jesus took the punishment of sin upon Himself in order to dismantle the devil's power. You now have the authority to destroy the works of the enemy because you have been purchased by the blood of Jesus. 1 John 3:8-9 (ESV) tells us, "Whoever makes a practice of sinning is of the devil, for the devil has been sinning from the beginning. The reason the Son of God appeared was to destroy the works of the devil. No one born of God makes a practice of sinning, for God's seed abides in him; and he cannot keep on sinning, because he has been born of God."

Right now the eternal seed of God is planted deep in the soil of your heart. Every day it is growing. This seed comes from Israel. This seed is Jewish seed. This seed is the Holy Spirit. As we continue to walk in faith, the works of the devil are being destroyed. Every time you choose to love, even when others are being hateful, you are destroying the devil's work of discord. This life giving seed is available to anyone who places their faith in Jesus Christ for salvation. Jesus tells us in John 12:24-25 (NIV), "Very truly I tell you, unless a kernel of wheat falls to the ground and dies, it remains only a single seed. But if it dies, it produces many seeds. Anyone who loves their life will lose it, while anyone who hates their life in this world will keep it for eternal life."

To be Jewish on the inside means you must die to your old self and choose to follow Jesus Christ. This is the only way to salvation and eternal life. It is the best way and the only way to live as Christians. The world will leave you hopeless and disappointed. The world will never fully satisfy, because this world and all that is in it is temporary. If you want to grow in the things of God, you must die to yourself. It is when you truly surrender to the Lord that He can begin to show you dreams and visions from above. He can show you the better life.

The better view is the heavenly view. When we choose to focus on the things above, that is Heaven, then the things of this world will seem trivial in comparison. All that we see in this world is merely a shadow of what is above. Even Jerusalem, as beautiful and glorious as she is, is only a shadow and a copy of the heavenly Jerusalem (Hebrews 12:22). As you pray for Israel and for the peace of Jerusalem, remember the battle Israel faces is spiritual. Diplomatic ties and military might are only a reflection and a response to what is happening in the spiritual realm.

Your prayers are powerful. Your intercession for the Jewish state could be the catalyst to bring fresh revival to the Holy Land. Never underestimate your prayers. When distresses come, the Lord is the one to whom we cry out. Like fishermen in the sea, sometimes the storms of life seem to overpower our ships. Psalm 107:27-29 (NASB95) says, "They reeled and staggered like a drunken man, and were at their wits' end. Then they cried to the LORD in their trouble, and He brought them out of their distresses. He caused the storm to be still, so that the waves of the sea were hushed."

Only Jesus can speak to the sea and calm the raging seas. Only Jesus can speak to the conflict in the Middle East and cause war to cease. Only Jesus can offer the shalom peace of Heaven that is out of this world. When Jesus looks down upon the earth, He doesn't just see Arabs, Jews, and Gentiles. He sees His brethren. He sees the children of God. His desire is that no one would perish but that all would receive the eternal life that only He can offer. As we pray for the safety and prosperity of Israel, may we also pray for salvation to all who dwell there.

Inwardly you are Jewish! You have been circumcised from the heart through Christ in you. Your Heavenly King will one day come again. He will establish His Messianic Kingdom that cannot be shaken. As the prophet Zechariah declares in Zechariah 14:9 (NIV), "The LORD will be king over the whole earth. On that day there will be one LORD, and His name the only name."

REASON SIX

Our True Allies in the Middle East

I am a Zionist to the core of my being. The longer I live the more I believe I was born to defend Israel, the Jewish people, and their right to not only exist but to thrive as God's chosen people. The fact that God chose Israel and the Jewish people does not offend my faith or my Christian beliefs. On the contrary, it makes me feel even more special to know I was hand picked by God from among the Gentiles to be in His big, happy, and blessed Jewish family. The truth is anyone who seeks after God and has been redeemed through Jesus Christ is now internally and eternally Jewish (see the previous chapter "Reason 5: Inwardly You are Jewish!").

The term Zionism originally came from a political organization established by Theodor Herzl in 1897. Herzl was an Austro-Hungarian writer and political activist who promoted Jewish immigration to Palestine. His efforts to form a Jewish state make him one of the early visionaries who laid out a practical platform for political Zionism. Herzl's work in promoting Zionism has made him known as the father of the State of Israel. Zionism is a movement to re-establish, develop, and protect the Jewish nation of Israel. Theodor Herzl is a modern day revolutionary in re-establishing the Jewish state. You and I have the opportunity to carry forward this vision of a flourishing modern-day Jewish state. Unfortunately, Herzl also encountered anti-Semitism during his day as a well-educated writer and playwright.

Today anti-Semitism still plagues not just the Middle East but the entire world. When I grew up learning about the atrocities of the Holocaust and World War 2 in school, I was baffled by how evil people could be. The hatred for the Jews and for Israel in particular was astounding to me. I grew up in a home that viewed the modern state of Israel as a miracle. Israel's rebirth in 1948 is evidence of the invisible hand of God at work. Today Israel thrives as the only democracy in the Middle East. Israel is our true ally in the Middle East. The Arab nations surrounding Israel are predominantly authoritarian regimes, meaning the government enforces strict obedience to the governmental authorities at the expense of any real personal freedom. Our Israeli allies stand as a beacon of democracy and of hope in the midst of the Arab world. Israeli democracy ensures freedom for the people, as officials are elected by the people.

Besides serving as a country that supports personal freedom, Israel also serves as a safe haven for the Jewish people, the growing Christian population, and other minority groups. I believe one reason Israel is able to offer freedom to its citizens more so than any other country in the region is because the Spirit of the Lord is so strong in the Holy Land. 2 Corinthians 3:17 (NLT) tells us, "For the Lord is the Spirit, and wherever the Spirit of the Lord is, there is freedom." The number of times my spirit was flooded by the presence of the Lord during my tour of Israel is countless. The archeological sites and various places we read about in the

Scriptures growing up can be seen in real life. Only in Israel can you touch the Western Wall, where the Temple once stood in all its glory.

By the grace of God, Israel has been restored in the midst of a land full of terror and anti-Semitic sentiment. Every day there are nations and people groups seeking to completely and utterly destroy Israel. Their hatred for Israel is spiritual. Because these people groups and surrounding countries do not know the Lord, they are carrying out the will of the devil. The devil hates Israel, because Israel is where God chose to establish His name. After King Solomon spent 7 years building the Temple of God (see 1 Kings 6:38), Solomon throws a huge celebration to honor the Lord and His Temple.

1 Kings 9:1-3 (NIV) says, "When Solomon had finished building the temple of the LORD and the royal palace, and had achieved all he had desired to do, the LORD appeared to him a second time, as He had appeared to him at Gibeon. The LORD said to him: 'I have heard the prayer and plea you have made before Me; I have consecrated this temple, which you have built, by putting My Name there forever. My eyes and My heart will always be there.'" The promise God made to Solomon that day has never changed. The eyes of the Lord have always watched over Jerusalem and the Temple Mount. It is no wonder the devil is stirring up Israel's enemies to launch missiles continually at this Jewish state of democracy and freedom.

The good news is God has His hand of protection over the land and the people of Israel. Israel has some of the most advanced technology and intelligence to defend herself. Israeli intelligence not only helps prevent terrorism at home, it also helps prevent terrorism worldwide. A great example of Israel's military resilience is in the development of Israel's "Iron Dome". The Iron Dome is an air defense system that intercepts and destroys rockets and fired artillery shells. This remarkable defense mechanism can stop missiles fired from 2.5 to 40 miles away, helping put a stop to the threat of destruction in Israeli populated areas.

Israel's development of life-saving technologies abound and will continue to as Israel prospers in the modern world. The Bible says that all who bless Israel will be blessed. We are to keep Israel in our thoughts and prayers, even if we are not a literal citizen and resident of the state of Israel. Our ties to the Holy Land through our faith in Jesus Christ are deep. The psalmist declares in Psalm 137:6 (NLT), "May my tongue stick to the roof of my mouth if I fail to remember you, if I don't make Jerusalem my greatest joy."

Jerusalem is the capital of Israel and the centerpiece of the world. What happens in Jerusalem impacts the entire earth, as she is the apple of God's eye. Several years ago I used to have recurring visions and dreams that pertained to the nation of Israel. In these dreams I would see an Israel flag and then a USA flag. In one of these dreams I saw myself standing with one foot in America, and the other foot was standing on the ocean; I was a giant size in the dream. At the time, I had been interceding for the nations and for taking the gospel to the nations. When I woke up I remembered the dream and the symbolism of it.

As believers we are called to be committed not to just our own country but all of the countries in the world. Jesus tells us in the Great Commission to share the gospel in all nations (see Matthew 28:19), not just the ones we think are suitable for our faith. Over the years, as I've built my ministry, I have always kept my sights on growing both domestically and abroad. While growing in America is easier and more cost efficient, I still remember the dream God gave me. The Great Commission calls me to not just keep both my feet in America but to also go to the rest of the world (like my feet standing on both American soil and the ocean in the dream).

My focal point overseas has always first been Israel. I have always had visions of an Israel flag on one arm and a USA flag on the other arm. The unique bond between the United States and Israel is one worth defending. I feel just as responsible for the wellbeing of the Holy Land as I do my own native country. The number of terror groups and countries who are against Israel is only going to grow in these Last Days. The Church should be so vocal and supportive about Israel and her right to exist that these groups who may not fear God should at least fear His Church!

We are a powerful Church, brothers and sisters, and a supernatural force to be reckoned with! One day all of the nations are going to be gathered against Israel. The prophet Zechariah declares in Zechariah 12:3 (NASB95), "It will come about in that day that I will make Jerusalem a heavy stone for all the peoples; all who lift it will be severely injured. And all the nations of the earth will be gathered against it." To put this verse in layman's terms: Israel is unbeatable even when the whole world is at war with her. As an American, I know it is in America's best interest to help fund and support Israel in the Middle East, as Israel has great intel on world terrorism because of where she is located on the map. As a Christian, I know it is in my best interest to support Israel because I want God's blessing.

Those who want God's blessing are going to have to wrestle for it. Just like Jacob had to wrestle an angel of God and ultimately walked away with a limp (see Genesis 32:25), so we are going to have to be bold and even stubborn in our support of Israel. The world is not going to like you for standing with Israel. The god of this world (2 Corinthians 4:4) and those who follow the course of this world are not for Israel, nor for the God of Israel. When you defend Israel, in the spiritual realm there is a big red "X" on your back. The devil is not going to sit back and let you chant, "Long live Israel!"

However, there is a blessing that comes for defending the Jewish state. God promises to prosper those who love Jerusalem (Psalm 122:6). As a watchman on the wall of Israel, you are called to pray for and call in the glory of Jerusalem that is coming before the Second Coming of Christ. Isaiah the prophet tells us in Isaiah 62:6-7 (NIV), "I have posted watchmen on your walls, Jerusalem; they will never be silent day or night. You who call on the LORD, give yourselves no rest, and give Him no rest till He establishes Jerusalem and makes her the praise of the earth." God's desire for Jerusalem is that this city would be the praise of the earth.

God's desire for you is that you would be a watchman on the walls of Jerusalem. His desire is that you would pray and intercede for His people in the Holy Land. Will you be one of God's watchmen? A watchman is defined as someone who keeps watch over a place at night in order to protect it from fire, vandals, or thieves. Jerusalem is surrounded by those who are seeking her destruction 24/7. Now more than ever we should show our love, support, and appreciation for those who are looking to the interests of Israel. If it was a dark hour when World War 2 and the

Holocaust were happening only a few decades ago, then imagine how dark of a world it would be if Israel's enemies were to succeed in their mission to destroy the only true sanctuary for freedom, democracy, and the Jewish people in the Middle East. It would be a very dark hour for the entire world indeed.

We need watchmen on the walls of Jerusalem. We need Israel to thrive and grow even greater in military might. Israel's protection is protection for billions of people from global terrorism. Pray for the Israel Defense Force, which is Israel's military. Ask the Lord to send divine wisdom and instruction over the leaders, to make them men and women who are like King David in battle. When Israel wins, we all win. If Israel were to fail, it would be a doom of darkness that stretches across the entire world. The prophet Isaiah declares in Isaiah 42:6 (NASB95), "I am the LORD, I have called you in righteousness, I will also hold you by the hand and watch over you, And I will appoint you as a covenant to the people, As a light to the nations."

Friends, Israel is a light to all the nations. The world is a much brighter place now because Israel is alive. Her people are thriving. The miracle of Israel is a bright light in the midst of a dark place. Despite her enemies who continually try to defame and delegitimize her as insensitive to humanitarian needs, Israel is very proactive in reaching out to the world in its times of distress. Like the United States, Israel is quick to respond to global disaster areas. Whether it is sending medical supplies, food, and other immediate needs, Israel has become one of the world's first responders when disaster strikes.

However, many of Israel's enemy continually try to spread lies and propaganda about Israel being an apartheid state that neglects her neighbors. Nothing could be further from the truth! Like the liberal media here in the United States, the media propaganda coming from other parts of the world that slander Israel is dictated by the devil and the spirits of the air. What we see and hear in the liberal news media is a false narrative. Half truths and spun up "facts" and figures are Satan's biggest tactics to deceive the world into hating Israel and the Jewish people. When Gaza and her terrorist friends launch missiles at Israel and Israel defends herself, the world says, "Pray for Gaza" - as if Gaza is the victim. When Israel responds with force (as they should), the world says Israel is oppressing her neighbors.

Friends, do not be deceived by the liberal narratives you read about and see in the media. Consider the source. If the source has no regard for the Lord or for His truth, then the source is going to be under the influence of the world. We are not worldly, Church. We are set apart. We see the real truth because we have the Spirit of Truth abiding in us. The devil can fabricate evidence all day for the world to digest. He can create illusions that seem real. If you are not seeking the Lord and reading His word, you are a prime target of the enemy to be led astray. Let us not be the ones who are led astray in the final days.

The ones who continually attack and threaten Israel are raised from birth to hate Israel and to hate the Jewish people. Anti-Semitism is a cancer that still plagues the earth. The good news is God has not forsaken His people. Even throughout the Holocaust, as atrocious as it was, God did not abandon His covenant people. The Lord may have allowed it, but God always gets the final say. King David declares in Psalm 37:9-13 (NASB95), "For evildoers will be cut off, but those who wait for the LORD, they will inherit the land. Yet a little while and the wicked man will be no more; and you will look carefully for his place and he will not be there. But the humble will inherit the land and will delight themselves in abundant prosperity. The wicked plots against the righteous and gnashes at him with his teeth. The Lord laughs at him, For He sees his day is coming."

As Israel does right by even her enemies, God will continue to restore Israel to her full glory. The nations who attach themselves to her are going to partake of her rich root (Romans 11:17). Those who come against the Jewish homeland and falsely accuse her will be cut off from God's blessings. Recently a radical left political group, Black Lives Matter, made a public display of demonstrations across the country. When this group resurfaced a few years after chanting, "Death to cops!", I knew by the Spirit that this political group was up to no good. Churches, ministers, and most all of the world was grossly deceived by the Black Lives Matter message.

On the surface, the devil used the guise of racism to promote the demonic agendas of Black Lives Matter. I immediately spoke out against this racially divisive, and even violent, political group that many were being sucked into by lies and false narratives. I faced tremendous backlash for speaking out strongly against Black Lives Matter (BLM) on their "Blackout Tuesday" debut, as the hate group claimed they were "only" protesting racism and police brutality in the streets. The truth is this political group also claims Israel is an "apartheid state" and supported the Boycott, Divestment, and Sanctions (BDS) movement against Israel. I was nauseated on "Blackout Tuesday", as I knew this ploy was funded by some very evil people, and they had the liberal news media and corporate America in their back pocket to shove this false message down the world's throat.

I knew by the Spirit that Tuesday was a very dark and evil day. The Lord showed me many visions. One vision God showed me was a huge demonic principality that looked like a black dragon, and young people in particular were being coerced into hopping on the dragon's back. The dragon had a cup full of black liquid that was to intoxicate its riders. As these deceived participants of the dragon rode, they became drunk on the dragon's cup of deception. They began to chant what the dragon told them to chant. This dragon was the spiritual force that was leading the Black Lives Matter movement. Towards the end of the vision I heard the dragon turn his face from waging war across the United States and said, "Come now, let us make war with Israel!" Those who rode along the dragon went off with him to fight against Israel.

The vision was so powerful and detailed that I knew the Spirit of God was showing me just how evil the spiritual forces behind these political movements were. As mainstream ministers, CEOs, and leaders stood behind Black Lives Matter, I knew Satan had pulled off one of the greatest deceptions of our time. People were supporting and funding great demonic activity. As I researched further into just how deep BLM's ties were to other groups, I quickly discovered that the BLM had ties to Hamas, one of the worst terror groups in the Middle East. Hamas hates Israel. Hamas is the political and militant organization in the Gaza Strip. Hamas is the terror group that trains children to kill Jews and to destroy Israel.

Hamas celebrated when Black Lives Matter made their debut on Blackout

Tuesday. They carried BLM signs and rejoiced, and of course they did. BLM is a friend of the terrorist agenda: "Destroy Israel. Boycott, divest, and sanction Israel." I speak out strongly against BLM because so many have been deceived by their lies and loud voice. If you support BLM or the BDS movement, you are an enemy of Israel, and therefore, an enemy of God. You cannot wine and dine with the devil and his dark agendas and follow God also. You are either with God, or you are against Him. We are living in a time where the line in the sand is being drawn. Everyone must choose who they are going to follow and serve.

Not only is BLM a Jewish hate group, they also are in strong support of aborting and murdering unborn children. Here in the United States, one way you can defend Israel is by simply standing against Black Lives Matter and those who are partnered with them. Their charter is full of godless agendas. Like the dragon in my vision, the cup of intoxicating poison BLM offers is something every true believer should steer clear of. The same is true with the Boycott, Divest, and Sanctions (BDS) movement. There are churches and certain denominations that support the BDS movement. If you know any who do, it is time to disassociate with such organizations. They are not walking with God or listening to His Spirit.

The truth is God is going to deal with those who are partnered together against Israel. When judgment day came for Sodom and Gomorrah only three people made it out alive. We don't know the day nor the hour when God is going to deal with these political and social groups that are promoting such godless agendas, but it will come. Like with Sodom and Gomorrah, it could come very quickly and with little to no notice. It is so important that we keep our ears tuned in to the Holy Spirit and keep our minds and hearts filled with the Word of God. As Christians, we are called to disassociate with political groups that promote ungodliness. We are called to support political groups and organizations that are advancing God's kingdom initiatives (like defending Israel's right to the land in Palestine and the rights of unborn children).

In the Spirit, we need to strap on our military boots and advance against these demonic forces attacking the Holy Land. We are God's children, called to go to war in the Spirit. I believe in the coming days we are going to see massive breakthroughs in Israel. I believe a spiritual revival is coming that is going to sweep through the Holy Land and even the entire Middle East! In the meantime, there is a war to be fought on our knees. It can only be won through prayer, worship, and fasting. It can only be won when God's people cry out for Israel's freedom in a world that stands against her.

During the civil unrest in the United States that was plotted, planned, and broken out by Black Lives Matter and by the evil forces behind this politically and demonically inspired movement, the Lord showed me another vision while I was driving through the country. In this vision I saw light snakes and dark snakes slithering along in front of me going in all directions. These snakes were too numerous to count, and they were slithering all over the land. The Lord showed me the serpents of light represented Christians who were as shrewd as serpents and gentle as doves (like Christian political leaders) and, and the darkened snakes were evil men and women spreading lies and false narratives (like corrupt politicians and liberal news pundits). I saw the light snakes going out of my spirit declaring truth all over the land, and they were at war with the darkened snakes.

Jesus tells His disciples in Matthew 10:16 (NLT), "Look, I am sending you out as sheep among wolves. So be as shrewd as snakes and harmless as doves." We are living in a world full of wolves. As much as we would like to think everyone is going to Heaven one day, the truth is there are many who are not. Jesus tells us in Matthew 7:13-14 (NIV), "Enter through the narrow gate. For wide is the gate and broad is the road that leads to destruction, and many enter through it. But small is the gate and narrow the road that leads to life, and only a few find it." Jesus then warns us in the next verse saying, "Watch out for false prophets. They come to you in sheep's clothing, but inwardly they are ferocious wolves." (Matthew 7:15 NIV)

There are more false prophets in the world today than ever before. There are so many voices and so many opinions being spread 24/7 through the airwaves. Whenever the truth is spoken, these talking heads are raging on the inside because the truth is not in them. The light offends their darkened spirit. That's why people rage against Israel and malign the Jewish homeland. Because there is so much malice towards Israel and towards the truth of God, it is important to be a Matthew 10:16 disciple! If we are not careful in how we handle dealing with those who are of the world, they will attack us like a wolf attacks a sheep in the open field.

We must be smart, Church. We are not dealing with innocent lambs in the world, especially when it comes to Israel's rightful role in it. We are dealing with vicious and ungodly wolves. Their master is the devil, and they are going about his business (whether they realize it or not). While we can and should pray for our enemies, we also need to be aware that not everyone is for us, nor for the God Who lives in us. One time God sent me a dream while I was staying in Los Angeles. I had recently published my first book, Tasting the Goodness of God, and I had a book signing scheduled at the local bookstore that weekend in Malibu.

In the dream I saw a snake floating through the sky. Then I saw another snake made of bronze coming from the opposite end of the sky that swallowed up the first snake. Right when I woke up I was alarmed and began to ponder what the dream meant. Later that day as I drove over the mountains into Malibu, I came across a newspaper stand after leaving a restaurant. The wind had blown open the newspaper onto the second page and there on The Malibu Times was a huge picture of my headshot with an article about my upcoming book signing! Right when I saw the huge picture I immediately understood the meaning of the dream I had.

From spending time in Malibu, I have learned some of the various beliefs people have. Unlike much of the Bible Belt, not everyone in Malibu or Los Angeles is a professing Christian. The Lord has repeatedly shown me a heavy spirit of witchcraft in the area, so I knew the first snake from the dream was the spirit of witchcraft coming against God's agenda to promote my first book. However, God raised up a more crafty and powerful bronze snake to swallow up the snake of destruction set to attack God's purposes for my book signing. The article drew several locals to the event, and the book signing was a great success. By the Spirit, I knew I had God's supernatural protection (and His bronze snake!) protecting me the whole time.

In the same way, God is protecting you from harm. In the spiritual realm God has spiritual beings that are swallowing up the plans of the enemy. When you step into the call of God on your life, you are unstoppable. The anointing on you is the same anointing that caused Israel to rebirth three years after the Holocaust. God had already established May 1948 on His calendar in Heaven as the time when He would raise the State of Israel back from the dead. I believe today God has some May 1948 moments planned for your life as well.

The key to going further and rising higher is by learning to stay in faith. When we start to grumble, complain, and become impatient, trouble is assuredly on its way. This is what happened with the Israelites in the desert when they got impatient. Numbers 21:4-5 (NLT) says, "Then the people of Israel set out from Mount Hor, taking the road to the Red Sea to go around the land of Edom. But the people grew impatient with the long journey, and they began to speak against God and Moses. 'Why have you brought us out of Egypt to die here in the wilderness?' they complained. 'There is nothing to eat here and nothing to drink. And we hate this horrible manna!'"

No doubt today it has to be difficult for Israelis living in Palestine. They are constantly under attack. They are continually maligned by their enemies. However, they continue to thrive and offer hope to the world. While Israel could sit back and complain, I believe they do just the opposite today. Israel is proactive in fighting for equal rights, fighting to end discrimination, working to end world poverty, and working to improve sanitation. In response, I believe the Lord continues to give Israel the cutting edge in technology and ingenuity because they are not playing the victim. They are branching out into the unknown and bringing about solutions for many of the world's problems.

When Israel in the desert with Moses complained, God allowed them to eat their own words. Numbers 21:6 (ESV) tell us, "Then the LORD sent fiery serpents among the people, and they bit the people, so that many people of Israel died." I don't know about you, but I would be terrified if I saw a bunch of fiery serpents in the middle of the wilderness next to nowhere! One reason God brought Israel into the wilderness was to test the people and to test their faith in Him as their Provider. Likewise, sometimes God will allow us to go through hardship, allow us to spend some time in the wilderness, in order to test us. Will we stay faithful to God even when things don't seem to be happening as fast as we would like? Will we keep seeking God even if we aren't getting our way?

When the Israelites realized they had sinned, they repented. Numbers 21:7-8 (NKJV) says, "Therefore the people came to Moses, and said, 'We have sinned, for we have spoken against the LORD and against you; pray to the LORD that He take away the serpents from us.' So Moses prayed for the people. Then the LORD said to Moses, 'Make a fiery serpent, and set it on a pole; and it shall be that everyone who is bitten, when he looks at it, shall live.'" The first step to getting back on the right track in life is to admit we have sinned against God. When we come to God and confess our sins, God has a solution. He has the answer.

Jerusalem's destruction in 70 AD was prophesied by Jesus Himself (see Mark 13:2). The reason God had Jerusalem and the Temple destroyed by the Romans was because of Israel's disobedience to God's prophets and to God's message. While reprimanding the teachers of the Law and the Pharisees, Jesus states in Matthew 23:37-38 (NIV), "Jerusalem, Jerusalem, you who kill the prophets and stone those sent to you, how often I have longed to gather your children together, as a hen gathers her chicks under her wings, and you were not willing. Look, your house is left to you desolate."

Because of the disobedience of Jerusalem, the house of Israel was left desolate for some 1,878 years. Then, all of the sudden, Israel came alive once again! When the Israelites repented in the desert, God gave Moses a solution. Numbers 21:9 (NIV) says, "So Moses made a bronze snake and put it up on a pole. Then when anyone was bitten by a snake and looked at the bronze snake, they lived." I believe the night before my book signing in Malibu, the Lord sent a bronze snake for me to look at and live. When I saw the bronze snake, it swallowed up the enemies plans to thwart my mission of spreading the gospel in Malibu.

When I look at the State of Israel today, I see a bronze snake defending her. The venomous snakes of this world may continue to strike and bite at Israel, but God has already set up the bronze snake. Israel will continue to go on and live. You and I are like the bronze snake. We can be a source of life and support for the modern State of Israel. Whether through diplomacy or through the developed free-market economy Israel has to offer, we can support Israel. Israel is one of the top 35 nations on the World Bank's ease of doing business index. She has the second-largest number of startup companies in the world after the United States, and the third-largest number of NASDAQ-listed companies after the U.S. and China.

This tiny nation of some 9 million residents is thriving! When we see how far Israel has come in less than 75 years of its re-existence, we should marvel at the goodness of God. The commanded blessing on the State of Israel today is unstoppable. When we begin to consider what a great blessing Israel is to the world, why wouldn't we want her to be our greatest ally in the Middle East? Whether economically, politically, technologically, or spiritually, we want to be connected with the chosen nation of God.

During my college years, I would frequently have divine inspiration as I went on my afternoon jogs. I thought about all sorts of things while jogging. One of the impressions I always had in my spirit during these times of exercise was my allegiance to both the United States and to Israel. I would see the two flags floating around in my mind. Often I would see a USA flag above my right hip socket and an Israeli flag above my left hip socket. It was a peculiar place to see flags, but I believe the Holy Spirit was showing me the hip socket because of the symbolism we see of Jacob's hip socket in the Scriptures.

You see, Jacob wanted the blessing of God. He desired to be the firstborn son. He wanted God's greatest blessings, so much so that he literally wrestled with an angel of God all night for it! Genesis 32:25 (ESV) tells us, "When the man saw that he did not prevail against Jacob, he touched his hip socket, and Jacob's hip was put out of joint as he wrestled with him." Jacob's hip socket represents holy ambition. It represents wrestling for the blessing. I believe God gave me the vision of the hip socket with the two flags because God has called me to fight both for my own country (the USA) and for the country where my faith began (that is, Israel).

The prophet Hosea speaks of Jacob's holy tenacity, saying in Hosea 12:3-6 (NIV), "In the womb he grasped his brother's heel; as a man he struggled with God. He struggled with the angel and overcame Him; he wept and begged for His favor. He found Him at Bethel and talked with Him there-- the LORD God Almighty, the LORD is His name! But you must return to your God; maintain love and justice, and wait for your God always." Jacob was desperate for more of God. I believe today God is calling Israel back. He has called them to return to the Jewish homeland.

You and I can be a part of this return. We can be a part of the Jeremiah 30:3 (NASB95) prophecy, which says, "'For behold, days are coming,' declares the LORD, 'when I will restore the fortunes of My people Israel and Judah.' The LORD says, 'I will also bring them back to the land that I gave to their forefathers and they shall possess it.'" In these Last Days God is bringing home the children of Israel. He has restored their fortunes before our very eyes. Israel has become an economic powerhouse that is booming in the Middle East. I believe we have yet to see all of the incredible technologies to be developed in the Holy Land.

I recently heard one pro-Israel commentator call Israel Silicon Valley "times twenty", as the technological advances coming forth are unrivaled. As a light unto the nations, Israel is loaded with innovation and life-giving ingenuity. A few years ago I remember watching a show, and in it was a Jewish man from the Holy Land who had developed a machine that gathered particles of water from thin air and used them to distill drinking water. The air was literally the machine's water source! "With these machines," the man said, "there would never have to be another drought. No one would ever have to go thirsty."

Israel is always looking for solutions to the world's problems. Whether it is in researching for new and better medical treatments, in producing drinking water from thin air, or in providing intel with other parts of the world about jihadists, Israel stands as a beacon of light in the darkness. She is the only democracy in a sea of tyranny. Israel is the first line of defense for the West. The tiny land of Israel, which is about the size of New Jersey, is what keeps jihad from coming to the West. They are on the front lines fighting for freedom against terrorist regimes like ISIS, Iran, Hamas, and Hezbollah, to name a few.

While the Christian population continues to shrink throughout the Middle East, Christianity is growing and thriving in Israel. Israel is a friend of the United States. Israel is a friend to the free world. Israel's enemies and our enemies are one and the same. Those in the Middle East seeking to destroy the free world - that is, those who support voting rights, freedom of religion, and equality - seek to wipe Israel off the map first. America is Israel's number one ally keeping this from happening. The United States sends around $3 to $4 billion in military aid to Israel every year. The US considers Israel a military foothold in the Middle East, and Israel certainly provides a stronger US presence in the region.

America also provides political support for Israel at the United Nations by using veto power to protect God's chosen nation. The US uses veto power to stop anti-Israeli nations from causing Israel harm on the political front. Of the 83 times the United States has ever used the veto, the US has used its UN Security Council veto power 42 times in resolutions relating to Israel. The United States has played a massive role in securing Israel as an economic and military powerhouse in the world today. It is no wonder

God has poured out blessings and favor on the United States like no other civilized nation in the history of the world.

Anyone who defends and helps establish God's people and God's land has the same promised blessing on them as the promise God gave to Cyrus the Great of the Persian empire. The prophet Isaiah declares in Isaiah 45:1-4 (NASB95), "Thus says the LORD to Cyrus His anointed, Whom I have taken by the right hand, To subdue nations before him And to loose the loins of kings; To open doors before him so that gates will not be shut: 'I will go before you and make the rough places smooth; I will shatter the doors of bronze and cut through their iron bars. I will give you the treasures of darkness And hidden wealth of secret places, So that you may know that it is I, The LORD, the God of Israel, who calls you by your name. For the sake of Jacob My servant, And Israel My chosen one, I have also called you by your name; I have given you a title of honor Though you have not known Me.'"

Why did God make Cyrus so great and powerful? For the sake of Israel, His chosen people. Why has God made America the land of the great and powerful? For the sake of Israel, still His chosen people. Make no mistake, the day the United States turns her back on Israel is the day God will turn His back on the glorious United States. Politically, we are in diplomatic ties with Israel. Spiritually, we are in covenant with Israel. When that covenant is violated, there are ramifications. The end to every nation who has ever come against Israel is never good. Babylon no longer exists, even as she was used by God to take the Israelites captive for their disobedience to His covenant.

There is no nation too great or too powerful for Almighty God to overthrow. This should be all the more reason to solidify Israel in our hearts and minds as our true ally in the Middle East. There is no greater nation to make one's ally than the nation of Israel, whose God is the LORD (Psalm 33:12). If not for the love of Israel, then out of the fear of the Lord all people from every nation should make Israel their number one ally. There has never been a nation like Israel to ever exist. She is the one and only of her kind. No other nation has withstood the test of time like Israel. For the sake of His promise to Abraham, Isaac, and Jacob, God will make sure the nation of Israel will always be here until the end of time.

The miracle and the resurrection of the modern state of Israel is here to stay, no matter how many rockets her enemies try to hammer her down with. Despite her neighboring enemies, who prefer to use international humanitarian aid to build things like terror tunnels instead of to help their own people, Israel will continue to seek peace where possible. When a group of people's hatred is even greater than their love for their own children, there can never be peace. When adults are willing to use their own small children as human shields on the top of buildings during an airstrike that they provoked, there is no peace.

For me, the dispute over the land of Israel is and always has been black and white. Every inch of land God said belongs to Israel in His Word belongs to the people of Israel. No government (no matter how great or small) and no terrorist group can nullify the Word of God. All who oppose Israel's right to the land that God has deeded to them are doomed to fail. Likewise, antisemitism cannot stand in the presence of the Lord. All of the hatred we see towards Israel and the Jewish people is satanic. It is a special kind of darkness that must be called out and fought against rigorously. If good people were to stand back and be passive towards this great evil, the next Holocaust would be inevitable.

Until Jesus returns, antisemitism and the demonic spirit that carries it is here to stay. We are going to be at war with the devil until his final day of judgment. The good news is we have the victory through Christ. We hold the keys to the kingdom of Heaven! (Matthew 16:19) As we can see the Israeli people to be our true allies in the Middle East, we can strategically pray for them no matter where in the world we may live. Those living in Israel are under constant attack. The propaganda being perpetrated against them is deceptive and misleading.

I've seen people I went to college with be deceived and misled because of false narratives put together by the Palestinians. The Palestinians use their own children as weapons of mass deception. They use their children as foot-soldiers in made-for-TV-riots and show pictures of dead Palestinian children to mislead the audience. Because the propaganda is so effective, Palestinian leaders have used systematic indoctrination to teach their children to hate the Jews and to embrace martyrdom. By placing their own children on the front lines during a battle for the cameras, the Palestinians can promote their anti-Israel agenda for the world to see.

As sick and twisted as these people are, we must pray for Israel's enemies. Satan obviously has his claws in them. To sacrifice one's own child for the sake of a false narrative fueled by hatred for the Jews is beyond repulsive. What's almost as disturbing is well-educated individuals, people that I know personally, are misled by the deception.

When two airplanes hijacked by al Qaeda terrorists took down the World Trade Center towers on September 11, 2001, I remember the day as if it were yesterday. I was (ironically) sitting in my high school history class, and the teacher carted in a TV for us to watch the news feed live. One of the towers had not collapsed yet. As we sat there in shock, I didn't know what to think. As time went on and the stories came out, America and MOST of the world grieved. Our Israeli friends grieved with us, sending us their deepest sympathies. After all, who understands being the victim of Islamic terrorists more than Israel?

What was Iran, the Palestinians, and their children doing? Dancing and singing. Celebrating "the victory". After all, marching while burning US flags and chanting, "Death to America!" is what they celebrate. Friends, the only thing stopping terrorism from striking again directly from the Middle East is Israel. Beyond all of our own brave US men and women in uniform stationed in the Middle East, Israel is our boots on the ground in the heart of an Arab region that despises the western world and all she represents.

Your Judeo-Christian principles are unwanted by the jihadist leaders who wish to dispose of Israel once and for all. If jihadists could remove Israel from the map, the next country they would target is the United States of America, or "big Israel". These Arab political leaders wishing to destroy Israel seek to destroy America also. We are one and the same to them. They would love to bring both Israel and America in subjection to their law and into subjection to their false god Allah, who is not a god at all but a demon from the pit of hell.

Under true Sharia (Islamic) law, women are restricted the freedom of movement, subject to the control of male guardians, denied access to certain jobs in government, and are forced to be veiled. Hands are to be cut off for stealing. Jews and infidels (that would include all of us Christians) are to either convert to Islam or be put to death. A true Koran believer agrees with these egregious and satanic teachings. There is nothing good or Godly about anything Islamic. It is the largest cult on the earth, and one that we must pray God redeems people out from under through Jesus Christ!

Until revival overthrows these Islamic jihadists, the free world must use military might and political prowess to protect itself from these demon-possessed, sick-in-the-head people. God loves the Muslims. He loves all people. Because God loves them, He does not want to leave them sitting in darkness serving the devil. God's desire is for revival to flood the streets of Saudi Arabia, Iraq, and Iran, for Koran's to be burned and the Word of God to be taught in the streets. The curse on the Middle East is real. The violence and horror stories we read about and see in the news is disturbing. The other heinous acts that we don't hear about, as the media reports what it wants and covers up what it wants, are perhaps even more troubling.

The good news is God's got this. He has His hand over the Middle East. He has not forgotten His covenant with His people. He has not forgotten the surrounding Gentile nations who are not serving Him. All nations are subject to revival. Before Jesus ascended into Heaven, He qualified that ALL nations were to have the gospel message preached to them. People of all nations and of all religions get a choice. Will we accept the free gift of Christ's salvation, or will we reject the message sent from Heaven? Jesus' arms are open wide to all who are in the world. The choice is ours.

As the geopolitical climate changes over time, one thing will remain true. Israel will still be our #1 ally on the planet. She will still be a beacon of hope and freedom to the rest of the world. The winds of change are coming to the Middle East. New peace treaties will be signed. Old peace treaties will be violated. There will be breakthroughs, and there will be breakups. The prophet Isaiah speaks of a time of peace when he declares in Isaiah 19:22-25 (ESV), "And the LORD will strike Egypt, striking and healing, and they will return to the LORD, and He will listen to their pleas for mercy and heal them. In that day there will be a highway from Egypt to Assyria, and Assyria will come into Egypt, and Egypt into Assyria, and the Egyptians will worship with the Assyrians. In that day Israel will be the third with Egypt and Assyria, a blessing in the midst of the earth, whom the LORD of hosts has blessed, saying, 'Blessed be Egypt My people, and Assyria the work of My hands, and Israel My inheritance.'"

All the nations of the earth belong to the Lord. God's desire is that all nations and kingdoms would serve Him. When nations are out of line, the Lord will strike them as He sees fit. He can use other nations to bring about His purposes. He can send destruction, and He can send life and healing. Isaiah 45:6-8 (NIV) says, "I am the LORD, and there is no other. I form the light and create darkness, I bring prosperity and create disaster; I, the LORD, do all these things. You heavens above, rain down My righteousness; let the clouds shower it down. Let the earth open wide, let salvation spring up, let righteousness flourish with it; I, the LORD, have created it."

The righteousness of God is coming to the Middle East. Those who do what is good and right, things that make for peace, are going to receive a reward from God in Heaven. Those who continue to promote terror and advance false religious ideologies are going to be punished accordingly. The Lord is going to shake the Middle East in these Last Days like never before. He is going to open up the heavens and cause His showers of justice and righteousness to flood down.

Whenever we question God and how He is handling the Middle East, we must remember God sees far beyond what we can see. Isaiah the prophet continues in Isaiah 45:9-12 (NASB95) saying, "Woe to the one who quarrels with his Maker-- An earthenware vessel among the vessels of earth! Will the clay say to the potter, 'What are you doing?' Or the thing you are making say, 'He has no hands'? Woe to him who says to a father, 'What are you begetting?' Or to a woman, 'To what are you giving birth?' This is what the LORD says, the Holy One of Israel and his Maker: 'Ask Me about the things to come concerning My sons, And you shall commit to Me the work of My hands. It is I who made the earth, and created man upon it. I stretched out the heavens with My hands And I ordained all their host.'"

The Lord has a perfect work He is bringing forth in the Middle East. Despite the terror, despite the violence, despite the horrors we see and read about in the news, there is still hope. Revival and reformation is coming. The Lord has promised us that in these Last Days He is going to reveal and pour out His Holy Spirit on all people (see Acts 2:17-18). The Holy Spirit can break through walls, terror tunnels, tyrannical leaders, and even major world religions. There is nothing that can stop an outpouring of the Holy

Spirit from Heaven when it comes!

Today there are more and more Messianic Jews living in Israel than ever before. As Israel's eyes begin to open to the revelation that Jesus is the Son of God and the Savior of the world, we are going to see massive global scale revival like never before. The King of Israel is coming back again. His return will be in the land of Israel. He tells us in Matthew 24:30-31 (NCV), "At that time, the sign of the Son of Man will appear in the sky. Then all the peoples of the world will cry. They will see the Son of Man coming on clouds in the sky with great power and glory. He will use a loud trumpet to send His angels all around the earth, and they will gather His chosen people from every part of the world."

Jesus is going to one day sound the loud trumpet from Jerusalem. Hallelujah! All people from every nation who call upon Him are going to be taken up with Him for eternity. He is going to return just as left, floating through the skies (see Acts 1:11). Jesus floated up into the clouds and was then seated at the right hand of God, while His disciples looked upward watching (Acts 1:9). The day He returns He will come back riding on the clouds in all His glory for all the world to see. What a glorious and marvelous site it will be! It will happen in an instant. Jesus tells us, "For as lightning that comes from the east is visible even in the west, so will be the coming of the Son of Man." (Matthew 24:27 NIV)

Israel, our true ally in the Middle East, is where the summing up of this age will occur. The whole world will be watching Israel when Jesus returns. For us to be alive as one of the first generations (and you may be the first generation if you were born before 1948!) to witness the miracle of

Israel's rebirth as a nation, we should be amazed and in awe and wonder of God's awesome power. The Lord has gathered His chosen people from all over the world post World War II. He has created a safe haven before the watching world for the Jewish people and for all people who have taken refuge there.

The Lord has established the Israel Defense Force as a powerful military that can physically defend the apple of God's eye. As an American, I am proud to be in an alliance with and in allegiance to the State of Israel. I am proud to be all in when it comes to defending Israel and the Jewish people. They are my brothers and sisters through what Christ has done for us. He has broken down the dividing wall (Ephesians 2:14). He has made us one people group through His blood.

When Israel thrives, we all thrive. To support Israel means to support freedom for all people. It means hope is alive for those who are surrounded by a sea of tyranny. All who visit and reside in Israel are free to be who they are. They are free to explore the Holy Land. They are free to see the living testament that our God is still alive in Israel.

REASON SEVEN

A Resilient People

Everything God said concerning the Jewish people is true. They are resilient. They have withstood the test of time. Whenever I encounter Jewish people, I am always amazed at their resilience. Many of their parents and/or grandparents never escaped the fences of Auschwitz or Treblinka, and yet they still carry so much hope and optimism for the future of the world. The Jewish people are world leaders, as they are the smartest people on the planet. There are none quite like the modern tribe of Israel, if you will.

How smart are the Jewish people? Since 1966, there have been twelve Israelis awarded the Nobel Prize. Over 20% of all Nobel Prizes (a little over 900 total in history since 1901) have gone to Jews, despite the Jewish population making up less than 2% of the world. The Nobel Prize is the most honorable award on earth for advancements in various fields like chemistry, economics, literature, and peace. Israel has more Nobel Prizes per capita than the United States, France, and Germany. If each country of the world represented a student in a classroom, and there are about 195 countries currently, she would be the smartest of the 195 students in the room. If there was a graduating class for the nations of the earth, Israel would graduate as the valedictorian.

Why is Israel so brilliant? Why is Israel at the very top of the class? Because God made her so. She is the head and not the tail. She is always at the top, and never at the bottom. (Deuteronomy 28:13) Seems unfair? I don't think so. I celebrate Israel's success. I've always believed and known from the Scriptures that success for Israel means even greater riches for the world (Romans 11:12). I love it that the biological descendants of Abraham, Isaac, and Jacob are thriving. I celebrate knowing Jews today are rising in the world like they did throughout the Scriptures (think Deborah, David, Solomon, Daniel, and Esther, to name a few).

The sense of nationality and unity Israel now carries from thousands of years of overcoming opposition and sheer hatred from the rest of the world is one that should be admired. When I see and hear how the Israel Defense Force (IDF) defends her borders from neighboring enemies through watching videos, looking at pictures, and even meeting IDF soldiers in person, I am so proud of them! The Holocaust victims who never made it would celebrate to see a powerful IDF defending Israel's right to life today. Furthermore, I am elated when I see US soldiers working and training with IDF soldiers to strengthen their combat skills.

Our US and Israeli soldiers are freedom fighters. They defend democracy and freedom as an example to the rest of the world. They are God's chosen ones to snuff out evil and physically liberate captives (Romans 13:4). They deserve our utmost respect. When I hear all of the hatred for Israel, the Jews, and the Western world that spews from the mouth of jihadist leaders and Islamic terrorist states, I thank God for giving us these brave men and women in uniform to defend us. They are our greatest hope against today's tyrants and terrorists, as God uses them to blot out evil before it can fully surface.

Today Israel withstands persecution remarkably well. It is not unusual to hear about synagogues still being attacked. Vandalisms and shootings at synagogues around the world are not uncommon, unfortunately. When I visited Warsaw, Poland, where the early ghettos formed and early events leading up to the Holocaust took place, many of the synagogues had been destroyed. The Great Synagogue of Warsaw was one of the grandest synagogues to ever be constructed. It was the largest synagogue in the world at the time before an SS Nazi soldier blew it up in May of 1943. This last act of destruction was to suppress the Jewish revolt in the Warsaw ghetto, which was the single largest revolt by the Jews during World War II.

The Nazis celebrated the demolition of the marvelous synagogue, yelling, "Heil Hitler!", as they pushed the button to detonate and destroy the Great Synagogue. Today, a skyscraper is in its place, which is mostly office space. Few remaining Jews visited or returned to Warsaw after the Holocaust. While I visited Warsaw (see "Reason 3 - Because Seeing is Believing"), the aftermath of the shock of war and the horrors of the Holocaust still linger in the air. Ironically, the skies were very cloudy and rainy on the days we toured the ghettos and listened to the horror stories that took place in Poland that week.

While Warsaw serves as a reminder of how dark evil truly is, my trip to Israel by catching the red-eye overnight to Tel Aviv was quite the opposite. In contrast, Israel is full of hustle and bustle. Excitement and beauty abound in the land of Israel! Seeing God's chosen people in their homeland, with plenty of armed forces for protection, displays the resilience of the Jewish people. The stark differences between Warsaw and the cities we visited in Israel were astounding. While the Jews were not mobilized, nor well-equipped, to defend themselves against the Nazi armies during World War II, they certainly are now!

Furthermore, Israel has a big brother - that is, the United States of America - guarding, funding, and ensuring Israel stands strong in her rightful place in the Middle East. Because the United States has helped ensure Israel's prosperity and protection over the past century, God has poured out His favor and unprecedented blessings on us. The Lord has used the greatest nation on earth to help restore the Jewish people to their ancestral homeland. Today Israel is armed with a powerful military. Israel is toppling towers of terrorist headquarters by military force. They are obliterating terror tunnels to bits, as modern-day "little Hitlers" seek to harm more Israeli citizens.

The forces of darkness are unable to overthrow the Jewish people and their place in the world. I believe one reason the Jewish people are so resilient is because the Church has begun to pray for this group of people to be restored like never before. The Holocaust was so appalling and disgusting, as the Jews were specifically targeted and rounded up by the Nazis from all people groups of the world, that it served as a wake up call and sounding board for the Church to not only begin to pray for the Jews but to also take action to protect them. The rebirth of Israel in 1948 was not easy for the early Jewish immigrants. Resources were limited and the Arabs abhorred the Zionist movement.

However, God never forgot about His chosen people. In the last century, His people have begun to return home. The days of the widespread Diaspora have been slowly coming to an end as the modern State of Israel continues to grow stronger. From 1948 to 1951, the number of Jewish immigrants more than doubled the Jewish population in Israel. As immigrants arrived from the world over, Israel began to build its own economy with employment opportunities. An education system was set up to meet the needs of children from diverse backgrounds.

One of the most miraculous rebirths from Israel in this era is the rebirth of the Hebrew language. The Hebrew language dates back to over 3,000 years. Until 150 years ago, the Hebrew language wasn't a spoken language. For centuries Hebrew was basically a dormant language. It was primarily used during religious ceremonies and in the study of Hebrew liturgy but not in daily life by the Diaspora. The language came back to life under the divinely inspired vision of linguist Eliezer Ben Yehuda. Yehuda came to Israel in 1891 with the dream to bring the ancient Hebrew language into a modern form. Furthermore, he made it his mission to ensure every Israeli home spoke in the Hebrew language.

Ben Yehuda came to realize his dream after pushing to make Hebrew the language of instruction in Israeli schools. He also expanded the Hebrew vocabulary for modern day words, created the first modern Hebrew dictionary, and edited early Hebrew newspapers. God used Yehuda to restore the Jewish State of Israel in all its fullness, which includes the

Hebrew language. When the Lord stirred up the entire planet during World War I and World War II, He was preparing the world for the new and restored land of Israel. While historians may not teach that the modern world wars had everything to do with God's chosen people, as believers we know Israel is the apple of God's eye. We know the regeneration of Israel is not a historical coincidence or happenstance.

The prophet Ezekiel prophesied thousands of years ago that this day was coming. Ezekiel declares in Ezekiel 36:8-12 (NLT), "But the mountains of Israel will produce heavy crops of fruit for My people—for they will be coming home again soon! See, I care about you, and I will pay attention to you. Your ground will be plowed and your crops planted. I will greatly increase the population of Israel, and the ruined cities will be rebuilt and filled with people. I will increase not only the people, but also your animals. O mountains of Israel, I will bring people to live on you once again. I will make you even more prosperous than you were before. Then you will know that I am the Lord. I will cause My people to walk on you once again, and you will be their territory. You will never again rob them of their children."

The population of Israel has skyrocketed since 1948. In 1948, the population of Israel was 806,000 people. Today the Israeli population is over 9 million. This tenfold increase in population is prophecy being fulfilled before our very eyes! Also, as another fulfillment of Ezekiel's prophecy, Israel is considered a "high income" country, most recently rising to one of the top 20 wealthiest countries on earth based on GDP per capita. The resilience of the Jewish state is remarkable. This modern septuagenarian country has risen dramatically through the ranks as one of the greatest countries in the world.

Ezekiel's promise to Israel is also one that we can hold on to for ourselves. The symbolism of Ezekiel 36 - that is, of returning home - can be applied to anyone who returns to God. When we turn from our sins and from living only for ourselves and turn to God, He promises to bless us. He can take the broken, destructive parts of our lives and make our souls prosper with "heavy crops" of blessing (Ezekiel 36:8). He can mend our hearts and make them whole again (Psalm 147:3). He can make us even more prosperous than we ever were before (Ezekiel 36:11). What we have seen in Israel's restoration over the last seven decades is not only something to marvel at but to also take to heart as a promise from God for our own lives.

Throughout history God has used the Jewish people to demonstrate His glory. God chose to use the Hebrew people to show the world He is the one and only true God. There is no other. It is estimated that the Egyptians had over 2,000 deities they worshipped. When God demonstrated His great power over Egypt with the ten plagues, all the nations learned to fear the God of Israel above all other so-called gods. The world learned very quickly that the God of Israel was far greater than all the gods of Egypt. When Israel drove out the inhabitants of Canaan, it became known that the God of Israel was greater than all other gods of the earth.

Psalm 78:54-55 (NIV) tells us, "And so He brought them to the border of His holy land, to the hill country His right hand had taken. He drove out nations before them and allotted their lands to them as an inheritance; He settled the tribes of Israel in their homes." As believers, we know there is only one God. When God settled Israel in the holy land, then drove them out by way of exile for their disobedience years later, He demonstrated His righteousness as the Father of Israel. However, it is one thing for God to punish and correct Israel as His child, but it is quite another when pagan nations start to treat Israel, God's chosen nation, with hatred and disdain.

When terrorist groups like Hamas vow to wipe Israel off the map in the name of Islam, God does not take these threats lightly. When ungodly Presidents like Barack Obama and Joe Biden use hardworking Americans' taxpayer money to fund terrorist countries, who then use much of those American funds to build missiles and terror tunnels to attack God's chosen people, God does not sit by idly and turn a blind eye. He has an answer for terrorist groups, Barack Obama, Joe Biden, and all who, by their actions, show that they despise God, His Word, and His people. Eternal punishment is coming for these people who refuse to repent, who have darkened their hearts and chosen to serve the devil.

The Apostle Jude describes these types of evil people well when he says in Jude 1:11-16 (NKJV), "Woe to them! For they have gone in the way of Cain, have run greedily in the error of Balaam for profit, and perished in the rebellion of Korah. These are spots in your love feasts, while they feast with you without fear, serving only themselves. They are clouds without water, carried about by the winds; late autumn trees without fruit, twice dead, pulled up by the roots; raging waves of the sea, foaming up their own shame; wandering stars for whom is reserved the blackness of darkness forever. Now Enoch, the seventh from Adam, prophesied about these men also, saying, 'Behold, the Lord comes with ten thousands of His saints, to execute judgment on all, to convict all who are ungodly among them of all their ungodly deeds which they have committed in an ungodly way, and of all the harsh things which ungodly sinners have spoken against Him.' These are grumblers, complainers, walking according to their own lusts; and they mouth great swelling words, flattering people to gain advantage."

The good news is God has given Israel the ability and the ammunition to continue to thrive, despite these evil leaders who do not have Israel's best interest at heart. When President Donald J. Trump declared Jerusalem to be the capital of Israel and to move the United States Embassy from Tel Aviv to Jerusalem on December 6, 2017, the angels of Heaven rejoiced! Like with King Cyrus, God used President Trump to further His own divine agenda to strengthen Jerusalem as the true capital of Israel in these Last Days. Even though ungodly leaders have refused to acknowledge God's Word or God's purposes for Israel, God touched President Trump's heart to obey His Word.

Great treasures await Donald Trump in Heaven for the many different ways in which he has honored God and His Word. Not so much for the other two US Presidents who have shown complete disregard for God, for His people, and for His Holy Word. Fortunately, the resilience of Israel continues to shine, regardless of who the US President is. The Scriptures say in Proverbs 29:2 (NLT), "When the godly are in authority, the people rejoice. But when the wicked are in power, they groan." One of the greatest blessings in modern Israel is their Prime Minister Benjamin Netanyahu. Netanyahu has navigated difficult waters as the most powerful leader in the State of Israel.

Benjamin Netanyahu won the Israeli elections in 1996, becoming both the youngest person in history as an Israeli Prime Minister and the first Prime Minister to be born in Israel. Today Benjamin, or "Bibi", is the longest serving Israeli Prime Minister in its history. Bibi has shown tremendous resilience as a political leader in the world, building allies and political goodwill with nations all over the world. His world-class leadership can be attributed to his ability to judge character and to communicate the truth with clarity while surrounded by people who are violent and insane. It is no surprise that Netanyahu was in a very good personal and diplomatic relationship with Donald Trump, and he has had understandable barriers in his relationships with both Barack Obama and Joe Biden.

Netanyahu has tactfully and successfully stood his ground in dealing with terrorists and jihadist-driven attacks on the Israeli people. When Obama signed the Iran Nuclear Deal giving the world's leading sponsor of terrorism over $100 billion of cash that had once been rightfully frozen, Netanyahu and Spirit-filled believers all over the world adamantly stood against it. Of course, the funds have since then been inappropriately misallocated by the Islamic terrorist nation. On May 8, 2018, President Donald Trump withdrew the United States from the catastrophic Iran Nuclear Deal, as it was obvious Iran was not honoring its terms (which Netanyahu knew Iran never would before it ever passed).

Today, Joe Biden is working on renewing the Iran Nuclear Deal, as can be expected from a godless leader. Biden has followed in the dark footsteps of his Democratic predecessor Barack Obama. Undermining Israel and Netanyahu, Biden is already trying to dictate to Netanyahu on how to handle Hamas, terror tunnels, and the Palestinians. Fortunately, Bibi is no fool. He has dealt with an evil US leader before (namely, Barack

Obama). I have full faith in Benjamin Netanyahu and the anointing God has bestowed upon him to continue to navigate Israel to further safety and prosperity in the coming days.

The truth is Israel is immovable. The Israelis are resilient because they have God's divine hand of protection over them. The prophet Amos declares in Amos 9:15 (NIV), "'I will plant Israel in their own land, never again to be uprooted from the land I have given them,' says the LORD your God." God has commanded Israel to stay planted in the Middle East. No rocket, no political alliance, and no terrorist can thwart what God has commanded. In early December 2016, a meteorological phenomenon occurred on the Syrian border when Israeli troops had recently repelled an attack by the terrorist group ISIS. An extraordinarily massive cloud full of dust and rain formed and began to serve as a giant hedge of protection between Israeli troops and ISIS. This weather phenomenon occurred in the exact same place on the Syrian border where ISIS had previously attacked just days before.

Observers who recorded the event attributed the phenomenon to divine intervention, which served as a buffer saving many lives from harm. The strange storm of dust, cloud, and rain did not cross the border fence into Israel. Instead, it sat like a giant barrier between ISIS and Israel. While the world may attribute this meteorological phenomenon to just time and chance, we know it was the invisible hand of God protecting His chosen people. The Creator of the world protected Israel then, and He is still supernaturally protecting them. The promise Isaiah the prophet once spoke still holds true today: "No weapon formed against you shall prosper". (Isaiah 54:17 NKJV)

Israelis and the Jewish people today are primarily peacemakers. When I speak with and observe Jewish people, one thing they do not like is war or violence. While Israelis will not hesitate to defend themselves when under attack, their desire is for peace. Prime Minister Benjamin Netanyahu has famously said, "If the Arabs put down their weapons today, there would be no more violence. If the Jews put down their weapons today, there would be no more Israel." This profoundly accurate statement by Netanyahu has been proven true over and over again. Israel has never vowed to wipe out entire Islamic nations and people groups in the name of Judaism. On the contrary, Israel's desire is for peace on all sides.

Israel's enemies' desire is for Israel's extermination. Sound familiar? Ever heard of a guy named Haman in the Book of Esther who wanted to destroy every living Jew in the Persian Empire? Ever heard of a guy named Adolf Hitler from Germany who tried to round up every living Jew he could and exterminate them? The Palestinian Authority, liberal anti-Israel hate groups (like Black Lives Matter), and other terrorist groups are of the same song, just a different verse. So what's the good news in all of this? The good news is their efforts are never going to work! Israel and the Jewish people have shown their fortitude and their resilience over and over again. No matter how many nations, people groups, or political leaders try to undermine and thwart Israel's right to exist in the world (because, as I've said before, Satan hates Israel and will use anyone he can to try and destroy her), they still have Almighty God on their side.

A perfect example of the world trying to delegitimize Israel's right to the land God said belongs to them is when Jordan illegally occupied part of the mandate lands reserved for the Jewish state. Jordan renamed the true name of Judea and Samaria in Israel to "the West Bank". Ever heard the phrase "the West Bank" in the liberal media? I cringe every time I hear the term. Why? Because "the West Bank" is the name Jordan, who tried to overthrow Israel, assigned to land that Biblically belongs to the Jews. The term "the West Bank" did not exist until 1950 - a term coined by Israel's enemies on the east side. Liberals, the "politically correct", Arabs, and Muslims love the term "the West Bank" because it undermines the true name of the land. God calls the land Judea and Samaria.

Why would Jordan try to rename land that we all know is called Judea and Samaria (as even Jesus called the land by its rightful name! See Acts 1:8)? Because Israel's enemies will do ANYTHING to erase the Jewish connection to the land. By attempting to erase its historical name from Judea and Samaria to "the West Bank" (a slap in the face from Jordan, as they renamed the land after illegally annexing it in 1950 until Israel took it back in June 1967 as a result of the Six-Day War), Jordan attempted to undermine Israel's right to their God-given inheritance. As time goes on, I believe Israel will continue to take back every inch of land God has said belongs to them according to His Word. While parts of modern Israel are still not fully restored to the Jewish state, eventually they will be.

What makes the Jewish people resilient is their ability to adapt well in the face of adversity, tragedy, and continual threats. While many Jewish people still have not acknowledged and received Jesus Christ as the Son of God and the true Messiah, which is the requirement for receiving the free gift of eternal salvation, many Jews are beginning to. A softening of hearts to the true gospel of Christ's salvation is already happening in Israel. The bridge being built between Christians and Jews today is perhaps stronger than ever before. I believe God's desire is to use the Church to support His plans for the Jewish State of Israel in a radical way in these Last Days.

God has given Israel much throughout the history of time. The Apostle Paul reminds us of their role in this world, stating in Romans 9:4-5 (NIV), "Theirs is the adoption to sonship; theirs the divine glory, the covenants, the receiving of the law, the temple worship and the promises. Theirs are the patriarchs, and from them is traced the human ancestry of the Messiah, who is God over all, forever praised! Amen." The reason the Jewish people continue to remain intact and to thrive over the millennia is because of God. God has preserved the Jewish people for a special purpose, even after many of them rejected Jesus as their Messiah.

The day is coming when all of Israel will be saved. The partial hardening of Israel will eventually be done away with (Romans 11:25), and Jesus will be recognized and worshipped as the eternal King of Israel! God still loves the Jewish people on account of the patriarchs (Romans 11:28), even despite their rejection of God the Son. God already chose ahead of time for the Jewish people to demonstrate His glory through them. Fortunately, God has grafted all people, Jews and Gentiles, into His household through faith in Jesus the Messiah. The two are made one through Jesus Christ (Galatians 3:28).

The most resilient Jew to ever live without question is the Jewish man named Jesus of Nazareth. Jesus, or "Yeshua" in Hebrew, is the entire purpose for all of humanity. Everything centers around Jesus. Why? Because Jesus is the Son of God. He is God in human flesh. He is the Creator of all things. He fulfilled every single Messianic prophecy written about Himself in the Old Testament (that is, over 300 individual prophecies related to the coming Messiah). As more and more Jewish people read the Messianic prophecies and then read how Jesus fulfilled every single one of them, the more they are coming to faith in Him!

The long list of why Jesus is the most resilient person to ever walk the earth abounds. From His miraculous birth to a virgin mother, to performing countless supernatural healings and miracles, to walking on water, to rebuking raging seas and thunderous storms, to multiplying a scarcity of food, to having an eternal transfiguration right before three of His disciples' eyes, to physically dying on a cross by way of Roman crucifixion then raising up from the dead in three days, to floating up into the skies while His disciples looked onward, just to name a few things, make Jesus the most resilient Jew and resilient human being to ever exist. He is so resilient that He is still alive because even death could not keep Him dead!

Jesus' list of accomplishments are so long that the Apostle John says in John 21:25 (NIV), "Jesus did many other things as well. If every one of them were written down, I suppose that even the whole world would not have room for the books that would be written." Even though we have many accounts of all the signs, wonders, and miracles Jesus performed by reading the Bible, there are still countless more Jesus performed that are not even recorded in the Scriptures. Jesus is God. The supernatural is only natural to God.

Not only is Jesus the most resilient Jew to ever live, He is also forever the King of the Jews. At the time of His birth, the wise men inquired in Jerusalem about Him saying in Matthew 2:2 (NLT), "Where is the newborn king of the Jews? We saw His star as it rose, and we have come to worship Him." Jesus was born as a baby in a manger, fully the Son of Man and fully the Son of God. The Apostle Paul explains in Colossians 1:15-17 (NLT) saying, "Christ is the visible image of the invisible God. He existed before anything was created and is supreme over all creation, for through Him God created everything in the heavenly realms and on earth. He made the things we can see and the things we can't see— such as thrones, kingdoms, rulers, and authorities in the unseen world. Everything was created through Him and for Him. He existed before anything else, and He holds all creation together."

When Jesus appeared on the earth, He was God in human form. There is nothing and no one who is more resilient than God. This Jewish man by natural human descent was the promised Messiah the Jews had been waiting for to redeem Israel. Not only has Jesus redeemed those who are Jewish, but He has redeemed those who are Gentiles from all over the world as well. As our Redeemer, Jesus has made us resilient through Him. This has given rise to one of the most popular Bible verses that we often hear quoted, "I can do all things through Christ who strengthens me." (Philippians 4:13 NKJV)

Some of the most resilient Jews to follow after Jesus' public ministry were His disciples, who became the apostles of the early church. Of the original twelve Jewish disciples chosen by Jesus, eleven went on to testify about Jesus as the Messiah with great power from the Spirit of Christ that rested upon them. These Jewish men, namely Peter (Simon), Andrew (Peter's brother), James (son of Zebedee), John (James' brother), Philip, Bartholomew, Thomas, Matthew (the tax collector), James (son of Alphaeus), Jude (also known as Thaddeus), Simon (the Zealot), and Matthias (who replaced Judas Iscariot, who betrayed Jesus) all remained resilient while spreading the gospel of Christ until the bitter end. I say the bitter end, because most of them died as martyrs for the newfound Christian faith.

These first twelve apostles had powerful public ministries, converting countless people to faith in Jesus. Not included among these twelve apostles is the Apostle Paul, who was a "Hebrew of Hebrews" (see Philippians 3:5) and wrote over half of the New Testament. Paul (formerly known as Saul) was one of the most zealous Israelites for the Torah (Jewish Law) of his day. He was so passionate about the Law as a Pharisee that he was one of the ones responsible for the violent persecution of the early Church. However, after a radical encounter with Jesus on the road to Damascus, Saul became Paul, and the rest is history.

Of all the early apostles, the Apostle Paul was arguably the most resilient of all. Paul himself tells us what he underwent as an apostle to the Gentiles, saying in 2 Corinthians 11:23-29 (ESV), "Are they servants of Christ? I am a better one—I am talking like a madman—with far greater labors, far more imprisonments, with countless beatings, and often near death. Five times I received at the hands of the Jews the forty lashes less one. Three times I was beaten with rods. Once I was stoned. Three times I was shipwrecked; a night and a day I was adrift at sea; on frequent journeys, in danger from rivers, danger from robbers, danger from my own people, danger from Gentiles, danger in the city, danger in the wilderness, danger at sea, danger from false brothers; in toil and hardship, through many a sleepless night, in hunger and thirst, often without food, in cold and exposure. And, apart from other things, there is the daily pressure on me of my anxiety for all the churches. Who is weak, and I am not weak? Who is made to fall, and I am not indignant?"

Paul is one of the most notable Jewish leaders to ever live. He underwent tremendous hardship in order to carry the gospel all the way to the heart of Rome, which was the most powerful and influential city on earth at the time. Despite all of the trials Paul underwent for the Christian faith, Paul still finished his race strong. Today we have Paul's letters to the churches so that his voice still speaks. Because of Paul's holy tenacity to preach the gospel no matter how difficult or violent things were, he never stopped preaching and teaching. In the end, historians tell us Paul was beheaded in Rome under the Roman emperor Nero (who had ordered for the mass execution of Christians at the time).

His fellow apostle Peter was crucified under Nero's fatal decree. However, Peter requested to be crucified upside down, as he was not worthy to die in the same manner as our Lord and Savior. There is nothing more resilient, nothing more noble, than to die for the one we love. Jesus, the disciples, and all the martyrs throughout history demonstrated their great love for God when they died for their faith. Jesus tells us in John 15:13 (NASB95), "Greater love has no one than this, that one lay down his life for his friends."

The greatest love ever demonstrated was in the act of Jesus dying on the Cross. The Apostle Paul writes in Romans 5:6-10 (NIV), "You see, at just the right time, when we were still powerless, Christ died for the ungodly. Very rarely will anyone die for a righteous person, though for a good person someone might possibly dare to die. But God demonstrates His own love for us in this: While we were still sinners, Christ died for us. Since we have now been justified by His blood, how much more shall we be saved from God's wrath through Him! For if, while we were God's enemies, we were reconciled to Him through the death of His Son, how much more, having been reconciled, shall we be saved through His life!"

It may be difficult to conceptualize, but Jesus died for us at a time when we were His enemies. Jesus accomplished what no other man could. Even Adam, who was made directly by the physical hands of God, failed to live up to God's standard of living and fell into sin. Through Adam's sin, death entered the world. Romans 5:14 (NASB95) tells us, "Nevertheless death reigned from Adam until Moses, even over those who had not sinned in the likeness of the offense of Adam, who is a type of Him who was to come." Adam was the first man to exist and is the first person in the long bloodline leading up to the birth of the Jewish Messiah.

The purpose of the Messiah's appearing was to undo what Adam's sin did. Adam's sin brought death and separation from God. Jesus' death brought resurrection, eternal life, and restoration with God. Romans 5:15 (NLT) says, "But there is a great difference between Adam's sin and God's gracious gift. For the sin of this one man, Adam, brought death to many. But even greater is God's wonderful grace and His gift of forgiveness to many through this other man, Jesus Christ." Restoring humanity to a right relationship with God is the single greatest act in history, and it was accomplished through the Hebrew man named Jesus (or as they say in Hebrew, Yeshua).

Jesus did what even the ancient Egyptian Pharaohs longed for but never actually obtained, which is eternal life. Jesus, and only Jesus, granted humanity the power to have eternal life through faith in Him. As we watch the invisible hand of Yeshua gather Israel under His wings in the Middle East during these last days, missiles and antisemitic political schemes launched at God's covenant people are going to fail. Israel is as David declares in Psalm 91:4-7 (NLT), which says, "He will cover you with His feathers. He will shelter you with His wings. His faithful promises are your armor and protection. Do not be afraid of the terrors of the night, nor the arrow that flies in the day. Do not dread the disease that stalks in darkness, nor the disaster that strikes at midday. Though a thousand fall at your side, though ten thousand are dying around you, these evils will not touch you."

The Messiah is coming back for His people. Jesus is King of Israel. He is the One whom Isaiah prophesied about when he said in Isaiah 9:7 (ESV), "Of the increase of his government and of peace there will be no end, on the throne of David and over his kingdom, to establish it and to uphold it with justice and with righteousness from this time forth and forevermore. The zeal of the LORD of hosts will do this." The eyes of the Lord are keeping watch over Israel and the Jewish people. In His zeal, the LORD of hosts will vindicate His people when they are mistreated, falsely accused, and attacked.

We are called to stand in the gap for Israel while she faces constant existential threats from her surrounding neighbors. Fortunately, God has blessed the Jewish state with a mighty military machine called the Israel Defense Force to defend herself with. Furthermore, Israel's economy continues to boom as overseas investors sow into the high-tech area (also called "Silicon Wadi"), which hosts over 8,000 active high-tech companies. Israel has earned the title "Startup Nation", as it has the largest number of startups per capita in the world with around one startup per 1,400 people. Around 300 high-tech US companies have a research and development presence in Israel, while many Israeli startup tech companies are invested in or acquired by foreign investors. As the Apostle Paul prophesied, the existence of modern Israel truly is riches for the world! (Romans 11:12)

As far as brain power, Israel is second to none. As I said before, if all of the countries of the world were a graduating class, Israel would graduate as the valedictorian hands down. Israel has the highest ratio of university degrees to population on the planet. Israeli citizens produce more research papers per capita than any other country in the world, as they are heavily invested in scientific research. Israel also has the highest number of engineers and scientists per capita than anywhere in the world. To add to all of their accolades, Israelis also have the lowest rate of diet-related deaths in the world. Bottom line: Israelis are smart.

The world needs Israel, but Israel does not need the world. Israel has superior technologies that meet the demands of the world in the new age we are living in. They have cutting edge technology to combat cybersecurity threats, water shortages, and Islamic terrorist threats. Israel is on the cutting edge in seemingly everything from medical breakthroughs to digital innovation to water conservation to food security. The resilient people of Israel are solution-oriented driven to address the issues of the world.

Why are the Jews so driven? Why do they continue to outwit their adversaries in the latest century and throughout the ages? The reason lies in their purpose given to them by their Creator. God created Israel in order to be a blessing to the entire world. Israel's global mindset stems from Heaven and flows onto the earth, much like the angels that climbed up and down Jacob's ladder (Genesis 28:12). Israel's greatest achievement was giving birth to Jesus, the Savior and King of the world. Beyond giving us the Messiah, Israel continues to give the world brilliant minds and world-class thinkers. The result has been advanced and unrivaled technology the world has never seen before.

These direct descendants of Jacob are fulfilling what God promised Jacob while he dreamed about the heavenly ladder thousands of years ago. Genesis 28:13-14 (NIV) testifies to this, saying, "There above the ladder stood the LORD, and He said: 'I am the LORD, the God of your father Abraham and the God of Isaac. I will give you and your descendants the land on which you are lying. Your descendants will be like the dust of the earth, and you will spread out to the west and to the east, to the north and to the south. All peoples on earth will be blessed through you and your offspring.'" God's purpose for the State of Israel is to bless the entire world.

The Jews are chosen and ordained to be a blessing to all nations. No wonder the devil fights so hard to oppress and destroy the precious Jewish people. Since Jacob had his dream while fast asleep in Bethel, the devil has tried to use countless kings and kingdoms to destroy the Hebrew race. The Egyptians, Persians (namely, Haman), Assyrians, Babylonians, Romans, Nazis, Palestinians, Arabs, and many other nations have attempted to oppress, and sometimes even completely wipe off the face of the earth, Jacob's descendants. This unexplainable animosity stems from Satan's ploy from the beginning to overthrow and overpower God Most High.

The prophet Isaiah tells us in Isaiah 14:12-14 (NKJV), "How you are fallen from heaven, O Lucifer, son of the morning! How you are cut down to the ground, You who weakened the nations! For you have said in your heart: 'I will ascend into heaven, I will exalt my throne above the stars of God; I will also sit on the mount of the congregation on the farthest sides of the north; I will ascend above the heights of the clouds, I will be like the Most High.'" Israel is where God chose to put His name above all other places of the earth. Satan's desire to demolish Israel is one more of his futile attempts to overthrow the Most High.

The eternal destiny of Satan has already been declared by Isaiah, when the prophet continues on to say in Isaiah 14:15-20 (NKJV), "Yet you shall be brought down to Sheol, to the lowest depths of the Pit. Those who see you will gaze at you, And consider you, saying: 'Is this the man who made the earth tremble, Who shook kingdoms, Who made the world as a wilderness And destroyed its cities, Who did not open the house of his prisoners? All the kings of the nations, All of them, sleep in glory, Everyone in his own house; But you are cast out of your grave Like an abominable branch, Like the garment of those who are slain, Thrust through with a sword, Who go down to the stones of the pit, Like a corpse trodden underfoot. You will not be joined with them in burial, Because you have destroyed your land And slain your people. The brood of evildoers shall never be named."

The irony is while Satan tries to blot out the name of God's people (like Hitler did during World War II), ultimately God will blot out Satan for eternity. The eternal destination of God's enemy is Gehenna, or the lake of fire (Revelation 20:10). All who call on the name of the Lord are saved from being cast into the lake of fire for eternity on judgment day. Revelation 20:15 (NIV) tells us, "Anyone whose name was not found written in the book of life was thrown into the lake of fire." The good news today is anyone can have their name written in the Book of Life. The only way to have your name written in the Book of Life is by receiving the free gift of the Messiah's salvation. Only in Jesus can one obtain salvation and enter into Heaven for eternity.

Revelation 21:27 (NLT) says, "Nothing evil will be allowed to enter, nor anyone who practices shameful idolatry and dishonesty—but only those whose names are written in the Lamb's Book of Life." God chose Israel to bring eternal life to the world. Jesus says in John 4:22 (NLT), "You Samaritans know very little about the one you worship, while we Jews know all about Him, for salvation comes through the Jews." God chose to show His righteousness through the Jewish people. He did not consult anyone when He decided to choose Israel to introduce both His righteousness and His salvation to the world. The Jews were chosen to steward the promises of God. They were chosen first to bring sacrifices that pleased the Creator of Heaven and Earth.

Jesus went to the Jewish people first when He preached the gospel message of eternal salvation in His name. The Apostle Peter tells the Jews in Acts 3:25-26 (ESV), "You are the sons of the prophets and of the covenant that God made with your fathers, saying to Abraham, 'And in your offspring shall all the families of the earth be blessed.' God, having raised up His servant, sent Him to you first, to bless you by turning every one of you from your wickedness." Peter's invitation to the Jews to receive Jesus as the

Messiah still stands today. We are all blessed because of the Jewish people. The sooner the world realizes Zionism is the greatest thing to happen in the 21st century, the sooner the world is going to see the greatest blessings in history.

The triumph of Israel in the modern era is remarkable. The State of Israel has fought through eight recognized wars since its establishment in 1948: Israel's War of Independence (1947-1949), The Sinai Campaign (Operation Kadesh - 1956), The Six-Day War (June 1967), The War of Attrition (1968-1970), The Yom Kippur War (October 1973), The Lebanon War: Operation Peace for Galilee (1982), The Gulf War (1991), and The Second Lebanon War (2006). The ongoing conflict Israel faces in the Middle East goes beyond what we can see with the physical eye. The battle we see is a mirror of the ongoing spiritual war for Israel's existence. I believe if we could see Israel with our spiritual eyes we would see Michael, the warring angel, and God's vast army guarding and defending this chosen nation. As the dragon wages war with Israel, he is no match for God's great army!

The Apostle John saw a glimpse of this spiritual war when he says in Revelation 12:1-2 (NIV), "A great sign appeared in heaven: a woman clothed with the sun, with the moon under her feet and a crown of twelve stars on her head. She was pregnant and cried out in pain as she was about to give birth." What John was seeing was the birth of the Messiah in Israel. The woman clothed with the sun is Israel. The twelve stars are the twelve tribes of Israel. The devil would love to devour Israel. If you want to know why there is no peace in the Middle East, blame it on the devil. He is a relentless dragon who knows his time before going to the lake of fire is short (Revelation 12:12). The devil will continue to rage against Israel.

While I do pray for the peace of Jerusalem and for the security of Israel in the region, the truth is there will be no lasting peace until Christ returns. The Apostle John continued to have divine revelation of Satan attacking the Jewish people (that is, Israel) when he goes on to share His vision saying in Revelation 12:13-17 (NKJV), "Now when the dragon saw that he had been cast to the earth, he persecuted the woman who gave birth to the male Child. But the woman was given two wings of a great eagle, that she might fly into the wilderness to her place, where she is nourished for a time and times and half a time, from the presence of the serpent. So the serpent spewed water out of his mouth like a flood after the woman, that he might cause her to be carried away by the flood. But the earth helped the woman, and the earth opened its mouth and swallowed up the flood which the dragon had spewed out of his mouth. And the dragon was enraged with the woman, and he went to make war with the rest of her offspring, who keep the commandments of God and have the testimony of Jesus Christ."

It might sound strange, but you (and all Gentile believers) are the "rest of her offspring" that John is referring to. Israel is the woman that the serpent is trying to destroy. Fortunately, the devil cannot defeat Israel because God is protecting her from him. Instead, the devil is now angry and at war with believers in Christ worldwide. Like with Israel, God is supernaturally protecting us from the raging dragon. We are all God's resilient people because we cling to the commandments of God and carry the testimony of Jesus the Jewish Messiah. We have to constantly pray and continually fight through all of life's battles because we have an adversary that is enraged with both Israel and with all who seek after God. The devil is not sitting still, and neither should we.

God's desire is that all would come to know Him. His will is that His resilience would shine through you. We are planted in this world to give glory and honor to the God of Israel. Psalm 113:3 (NKJV) says, "From the rising of the sun to its going down The LORD's name is to be praised." The end result of all that happens in this world is God will be glorified. He is our sustenance for all we need. John 6:32-35 (NCV) says, "Jesus said, 'I tell you the truth, it was not Moses who gave you bread from heaven; it is My Father who is giving you the true bread from heaven. God's bread is the One who comes down from heaven and gives life to the world.' The people said, 'Sir, give us this bread always.' Then Jesus said, 'I am the bread that gives life. Whoever comes to Me will never be hungry, and whoever believes in Me will never be thirsty.'"

Friends, Jesus is more than enough for all we are ever going to need. He is our Provider both in this life and in the life to come. The Bread of Heaven came to Israel and has been shared with the rest of the world. This Bread is sacred and holy. The Father's Bread is completely free of charge for all who come to Him. Jesus is the Bread from Heaven, sent to to feed Israel and to feed all of the nations. Now more than ever the State of Israel needs this heavenly bread, and I believe God is going to supply it. Just as God rained down manna from the skies for provision as Moses led the people of Israel into the Promised Land, so in these Last Days God is going to supernaturally rain down His provision in the Holy Land.

As Israel leads the world in these coming days, we have an opportunity as the Bride of Christ to participate with them. It is not a coincidence you were born in the 21st century, just around the time that the modern State of Israel miraculously formed. You are called to be in partnership with this beacon of freedom in the Middle East as a child of Abraham. You are called to stand up for Israel's right to exist and defend herself. You are Israel's watchman on the wall (Isaiah 62:6) as a follower of Christ. Whether through politics, Christian organizations, or your local church, you can be involved in a ministry that supports Israel and the Jewish people.

Furthermore, I believe you are going to experience more blessings in your own life as you dedicate your time and resources to advancing the wellbeing of the State of Israel as the Spirit leads you. You are being resilient when you take a stand against antisemitism. You are being resilient when you go against the crowd and do what is right in God's eyes. Your identity is not found in the world. Your identity is found in Christ. Jesus tells us in John 15:18-21 (NIV), "If the world hates you, keep in mind that it hated Me first. If you belonged to the world, it would love you as its own. As it is, you do not belong to the world, but I have chosen you out of the world. That is why the world hates you. Remember what I told you: 'A servant is not greater than his master.' If they persecuted Me, they will persecute you also. If they obeyed My teaching, they will obey yours also. They will treat you this way because of My name, for they do not know the One who sent Me."

You have been chosen by Christ from out of the world to come and follow Him. You are part of the inheritance and legacy of Israel. You are His royal priesthood, called into the house of God in order to serve Him. As you run your race, one day you are going to cross the finish line. I believe as you seek the God of Israel, you are going to finish this life strong like the Apostle Paul. Paul tells Timothy in 2 Timothy 4:6-8 (NLT), "As for me, my life has already been poured out as an offering to God. The time of my death is near. I have fought the good fight, I have finished the race, and I have remained faithful. And now the prize awaits me—the crown of righteousness, which the Lord, the righteous Judge, will give me on the day of His return. And the prize is not just for me but for all who eagerly look forward to His appearing."

As we all look forward to the glorious reappearing of our Messiah to Israel and the entire world, we carry the mantle for future generations. It is up to us to tell the next generation about the good news of Jesus Christ. It is up to us to inform the next generation about how important the State of Israel is in the modern world. As King David declares in Psalm 145:4-7 (NLT), "Let each generation tell its children of Your mighty acts; let them proclaim Your power. I will meditate on Your majestic, glorious splendor and Your wonderful miracles. Your awe-inspiring deeds will be on every tongue; I will proclaim Your greatness. Everyone will share the story of Your wonderful goodness; they will sing with joy about Your righteousness."

Conclusion

The reasons to support the modern State of Israel abound. Everyone has different opinions and viewpoints in regard to the Middle East. However, one thing remains absolutely true and that is God's Word. The Scriptures never waiver, nor change. Throughout the ages, God has never retracted His promises. When God makes an oath, it stands forever. Hebrews 6:12-13 (NKJV) tells us, "For when God made a promise to Abraham, because He could swear by no one greater, He swore by Himself, saying, 'Surely blessing I will bless you, and multiplying I will multiply you.'"

Knowing why we should support Israel is futile if we do not translate our knowledge into action. Like myself, knowing the truth about the modern State of Israel likely inspires you to want to take action. There are numerous ways you can be a part of what God is doing today in the Middle East. The first way you can support Israel is simply by praying. Prayer is free, and it only takes a couple of minutes per day to keep Israel in our daily prayers. Beyond prayer, which should never be underestimated, you can financially support ministries that are spiritually investing into the Holy Land like Jewish Voice Ministries International,

International Fellowship of Christians and Jews, and First Fruits of Zion.

If you are more political minded, you may want to be in partnership with political groups like Christians United For Israel (CUFI), the American Israel Public Affairs Committee (AIPAC), or the Republican Jewish Coalition. Beyond spiritual and political groups, you might also consider investing in publicly traded companies that are in the Jewish State. Attend a Messianic Jewish church sometime if you ever have the opportunity. Listening to and being around Hebrew Christians (Messianic Jews) is very enlightening, as they celebrate Biblical holidays like Pesach, Sukkot, and Shavuot. With over 1 million Messianic Jews in the United States who believe in Yeshua, or Jesus, this number is sure to grow as more and more Jews come to know their Jewish Messiah Yeshua as their personal Lord and Savior!

When I first invested in an Israeli company several years ago, God blessed me in return. Over the following months the Lord released a spirit of wisdom over me in handling my finances. My financial position began to radically change, and today I am in a much more secure position than I was before. The Apostle Paul says 2 Corinthians 9:6 (ESV), "The point is this: whoever sows sparingly will also reap sparingly, and whoever sows bountifully will also reap bountifully." When we take whatever seed is in our hands, whether that be our money, time, or skillset, and plant it into the work of God, over time we are going to reap a harvest of blessing.

Taking action should be our response whenever we hear about antisemitism and anti-Israel public policies in the news. It is when good people do nothing that evil is sure to prevail. James 1:22 (NCV) tells us,

"Do what God's teaching says; when you only listen and do nothing, you are fooling yourselves." God rewards obedience. He rewards those who respond to the call of His Word. It is when we fail to take action that we miss the opportunity for more of God's blessings. Serving the Lord is what lifts our souls and gives us great joy. Whenever I share about Israel with friends, family, and the church, my soul is always flooded with delight. Talking about the Promised Land is exciting!

Furthermore, we are living in an era where we have just witnessed the miracle of Israel's rebirth. Seeing this miracle should give God's people something to talk about. Israeli flags should be hanging in churches all over the world in celebration of what God has done in bringing back to life the modern Jewish State of Israel. We all can play a part in shaping the future of Israel. Israel is the birthplace of the Jewish people and the birthplace of our Christian faith. Just as a child is called to honor their parents who gave them life, so we are called to honor the land and the people through whom salvation has come.

For some 35 centuries, Israel and the Jewish people have stood as God's centerpiece in this world. You and I are a part of this long history in the making. As we give God our firstfruits, as we give God our very best, only then are we going to tase and see how good God truly is. Deuteronomy 26:9-10 (NLT) says, "He brought us to this place and gave us this land flowing with milk and honey! And now, O LORD, I have brought you the first portion of the harvest You have given me from the ground." All that we have belongs to the Lord. All that God asks in return is the tithe, which is the first ten percent of our income. When you give God the first portion of your resources, the first of your time and energy, He is going to give you far more back in return.

Participating in the advancement of Israel's wellbeing will be rewarded. Jesus tells us in Revelation 22:12-17 (NCV), "Listen! I am coming soon! I will bring My reward with Me, and I will repay each one of you for what you have done. I am the Alpha and the Omega, the First and the Last, the Beginning and the End. Blessed are those who wash their robes so that they will receive the right to eat the fruit from the tree of life and may go through the gates into the city. Outside the city are the evil people, those who do evil magic, who sin sexually, who murder, who worship idols, and who love lies and tell lies. I, Jesus, have sent My angel to tell you these things for the churches. I am the descendant from the family of David, and I am the bright morning star. The Spirit and the bride say, 'Come!' Let the one who hears this say, 'Come!' Let whoever is thirsty come; whoever wishes may have the water of life as a free gift."

As the Last Days that we are now living in draw to the end, Israel will be the focal point of all the nations. How you respond to Israel matters. What you do makes an impact that will last throughout eternity. Christ's invitation to receive the free gift of eternal life still stands for Jews and Gentiles alike. When you stand with Christ, you will not fall with the devil. When you stand with Israel, you will not fall with the rest of the world. It's why I have chosen to stand with Jesus. It's why I have chosen stand with Israel. It's why I hope you choose to make the right choice and stand with Jesus Christ. It's why I hope after reading this book you make the right choice and choose to stand with Israel too.

Take Action

"BUT BE DOERS OF THE WORD,
AND NOT HEARERS ONLY, DECEIVING YOURSELVES."
JAMES 1:22 NKJV

JEWISH VOICE MINISTRIES INTERNATIONAL

Mission: "Jewish Voice exists to transform lives and see all Israel saved. Our mission is to: Proclaim the Gospel to the Jew First. Grow the Messianic Jewish community. Engage the Church concerning Israel and the Jewish people. We carry out this mission through a many-faceted ministry that includes humanitarian medical outreaches, large-scale international festivals, congregation planting and leadership training, television, print media, digital channels, and speaking engagements."

Address: P.O. Box 31998, Phoenix, AZ 85046

Website: www.jewishvoice.org

INTERNATIONAL FELLOWSHIP OF CHRISTIANS AND JEWS

Mission: "The leading non-profit building bridges between Christians and Jews, blessing Israel and the Jewish people around the world with humanitarian care and life-saving aid."

Address: 30 North LaSalle Street, Suite 4300, Chicago, IL 60602-2584

Website: www.ifcj.org

FIRST FRUITS OF ZION

Mission: "Specializes in the study and teaching of Scripture from its historical, linguistic, and cultural context. Using the latest scholarship, ancient Jewish sources, and extra-biblical literature, we present a Messianic Jewish reading of the Bible and early Jewish-Christianity. We do this by publishing books, ebooks, magazines, journals, study programs, audio and audio-visual resources, and presenting new material through seminars, conferences, and guided Israel tours."

Address: PO Box 649, Marshfield, MO 65706-0649
Website: www.ffoz.org

FUSION WITH RABBI JASON SOBEL

Mission: "We want to add definition to your faith as we restore the lost connection to our ancient roots and rediscover our forgotten inheritance. By expanding our understanding of prayer and scripture to include ancient Hebrew and contemporary wisdom informed by the Spirit, we can enrich our perspective of Yeshua (Jesus), His teachings, and His disciples."

Address: 5062 Lankershim Blvd., Suite 3017 North Hollywood, CA 91601
Website: www.fusionglobal.org

CHRISTIANS UNITED FOR ISRAEL - CUFI

Mission: "As the largest pro-Israel organization in the United States, with over 10 million members, Christians United for Israel (CUFI) is the foremost Christian organization educating and empowering millions of

Americans to speak and act with one voice in defense of Israel and the Jewish people. CUFI's diversity across political, ethnic, generational and denominational lines maximizes our impact in communities, the media, on campus, and in our nation's capital. CUFI is committed to confronting indifference and combating antisemitism in all its forms wherever it may be found."

Address: PO Box 1307, San Antonio, TX 78295-1307

Website: www.cufi.org

THE AMERICAN ISRAEL PUBLIC AFFAIRS COMMITTEE - AIPAC

Mission: "The mission of AIPAC is to encourage and persuade the U.S. government to enact specific policies that create a strong, enduring and mutually beneficial relationship with our ally Israel. We engage with and educate decision-makers about the bonds that unite the two countries, and how it is in America's best interest to strengthen those bonds and help ensure that the Jewish state remains safe, strong and secure."

Address: 440 First Street NW - Suite 600, Washington, DC 20001

Website: www.aipac.org

REPUBLICAN JEWISH COALITION

Mission: "We seek to foster and enhance ties between the American Jewish community and Republican decision makers. We work to sensitize Republican leadership in government and the Party to the concerns and issues of the Jewish community, while articulating and advocating Republican ideas and policies within the Jewish community. We are committed to building a strong, effective and respected Jewish Republican voice in Washington and across the country."

Address: 50 F Street NW, Suite 100, Washington, DC 20001

Website: www.rjchq.org

ISRAEL MINISTRY OF FOREIGN AFFAIRS

Mission: "One of the most important ministries in the Israeli government. The ministry's role is to implement Israel's foreign policy, and promote economic, cultural, and scientific relations with other countries."

Address: Sderot Yitshak Rabin 9, Jerusalem, 9195022, Israel

Website: www.mfa.gov.il

U.S. DEPARTMENT OF STATE

Mission: "Leads America's foreign policy through diplomacy, advocacy, and assistance by advancing the interests of the American people, their safety and economic prosperity."

Address: 2201 C St NW, Washington, DC 20520

Website: www.state.gov/countries-areas/israel

ALSO WRITTEN BY
McKade Marshall

TASTING THE GOODNESS OF GOD

This book of 31 devotional thoughts is just the beginning of McKade putting into words, messages of hope and inspiration for every day of the month. May these words shared from his heart of transparency be a source of comfort, strength, encouragement, and growth in your own life as you turn every page.

BREATHE

Breathe is a Christian inspirational book filled with twenty-five different "mini-sermons", encouraging the reader to live out their dreams as they walk in faith. *Breathe* is filled with messages of hope, encouraging readers to go deeper in their faith journey. May these words shared from McKade's heart of transparency be a source of comfort, strength, encouragement, and growth in your own life as you turn each page.

FINDING YOUR KEYS

Finding Your Keys is about helping you discover and be reminded of the authority you have as a believer in Christ. Inside every believer are keys God has given us to use to unlock the supernatural power of God's Kingdom in our everyday lives. Just as the right key unlocks a door, giving you access to a protected room, so God has given us different keys - or spiritual truths - to unlock His supernatural power in our lives. It's time to start finding your keys!

www.ingramcontent.com/pod-product-compliance
Lightning Source LLC
Chambersburg PA
CBHW031317160426
43196CB00007B/563